Joshua and Me

By
David Shoots

TABLE OF CONTENT

INTRODUCTION

We all can say that we live in a tough world today as Christians. It is so easy to get caught up with the world, politics, world this and world that. We have everyday life things that we have to deal with, such as relationships, walking the right way with God, being a good witness, and dealing with anxiety and depression just like almost everyone else (except the walking with God thing, as that's only for Christians). The Power of the gospel is the simplicity of the gospel. It is the simple things that are so powerful: Pray, study your word, accept the death, burial, and resurrection of Jesus, love God, and love your neighbor as yourself.

I came across this story of Joshua in Zechariah. It was intriguing how the story depicts Joshua as a man who is dirty, muddy, unclean, being lied about, talked about, and put down by the enemy as he is presented before the Throne. I was amazed by the words of the Father for this man to be set free even though he was guilty. He was given things that he did not purchase, a place he did not build, and a relationship that he was not even close to being qualified to be in. Yet he was presented as dirty but made clean. This is salvation. This is the wonderful hope of all saints of God. In a very real way, we are Joshua. We are unclean, dirty, guilty, unruly, troublemakers, unfit, and just plain unworthy. I remember the hymn of "Love Lifted Me". The first verse goes:

I was sinking deep in sin

Far from the peaceful shore

Very deeply stained within

Sinking to rise no more

But the master of the sea

Heard my despairing cry,

From the waters lifted me

Now safe, am I

Love lifted me! Love lifted me!

When nothing else could help

Love lifted me

Love lifted me! Love lifted me!

When nothing else could help

Love lifted me

(https://www.google.com/search?q=love+lifted+me+lyrics)

What a beautiful picture of us. Salvation is often forgotten in our society. It is almost like it is taken for granted. It starts with the cross, as far as I'm concerned. We must never get caught up in things that take us away from the cross of Jesus. Prosperity is ok as long as it is spiritual. We should not be chasing things, but things should be chasing us. The 23rd Psalm tells us that surely goodness and mercy shall follow or chase us all the days of our lives. If our focus is on Jesus and His goodness, those things will be added to us. Seek ye first the kingdom of God and His righteousness, and all of these things shall be added unto you. Many people have this backward, believing that someone should be chasing the good life here. Sorry to burst your bubble, but even Christ tells us that we cannot take these things with us, so why build up for yourself all of these things like fine gold and silver? Instead, folks should look to the Hills, which cometh to our help. He tells us that we cannot serve two masters. Either you are chasing after things or chasing after God.

People must never forget that we are like Joshua. The person who, on their own, is dirty, filthy, full of sin with no hope. We must never forget the price Jesus paid for us to have life. We must never forget that we were lost. Remember that Christians were bought with a price. I think this can intensify our praise and worship. Knowing the price that was paid will keep this walk as weal walk with God. Of course, we must grow, walk in the faith, and be a witness, but it is the cross that makes all of this possible. This is what I want to address: the real walk afterward. I want to keep this as simple as possible. The reality of us is that folks are human. God knows our humanity and is aware of our humanness, frailties, tendencies, and the like. As a Pastor and a Mental Health Therapist, I would like to take us on a journey as both.

Every one of the chapters of the book will conclude with some reflective questions or prompts that you, the reader, can use for a more practical application of the lessons in this book. For this chapter, consider the following:

- What does "walking with God" mean to you personally?

- Reflect on a moment when you felt overwhelmed by the world. How did you navigate it?

- Write about your understanding of the "simplicity of the gospel." How does it shape your faith journey?

CHAPTER: 1

FORGIVENESS

Sermon

Zechariah 3

3 Then he showed me Joshua the high priest standing before the angel of the Lord, and Satan[a] standing at his right side to accuse him. ² The Lord said to Satan, "The Lord rebuke you, Satan! The Lord, who has chosen Jerusalem, rebuke you! Is not this man a burning stick snatched from the fire?"

³ Now Joshua was dressed in filthy clothes as he stood before the angel. ⁴ The angel said to those who were standing before him, "Take off his filthy clothes."

Then he said to Joshua, "See, I have taken away your sin, and I will put fine garments on you."

⁵ Then I said, "Put a clean turban on his head." So they put a clean turban on his head and clothed him while the angel of the Lord stood by.

⁶ The angel of the Lord gave this charge to Joshua: ⁷ "This is what the Lord Almighty says: 'If you will walk in obedience to me and keep my requirements, then you will govern my house and have charge of my courts, and I will give you a place among these standing here.

⁸ "'Listen, High Priest Joshua, you and your associates seated before you, who are men symbolic of things to come: I am going to bring my servant, the Branch. ⁹ See, the stone I have set in front of Joshua! There are seven eyes[b] on that one stone, and I will engrave an inscription on it,' says the Lord Almighty, 'and I will remove the sin of this land in a single day.

[10] "'In that day each of you will invite your neighbor to sit under your vine and fig tree,' declares the Lord Almighty." (Bible Gateway)

As a pastor, I've come across hundreds of intriguing passages in the Holy Bible. But, one story that really stuck with me: It was of Zachariah. One of the first sermons that I preached had to do with this character in Zachariah. I had never heard of this Joshua when I first found it. I realize how much of myself and Joshua were similar today.

First, let's note that the Joshua in Zechariah is a different Joshua that is his name's sake in the Old Testament book of Joshua. Joshua was the assistant to Moses, who led Israel across the Jordan River out of the hands of the Egyptians into the promised land at or around 1400 BC. The Joshua that is mentioned in Zechariah chapter 3 was a Levi, a descendant of Aaron at or around 538 BC. Joshua's name appears as "Jeshua," and it's listed as one of the first of those returning from Babylon, found in Nehemiah Chapter 7. Upon further study, the prophet Haggai also refers to the high priest Joshua found in Haggai 1:1: *In the second year of King Darius, on the first day of the sixth month, the word of the Lord came through the prophet Haggai to Zerubbabel son of Shealtiel, governor of Judah, and to Joshua son of Jozadak,[a] the high priest:* <u>Haggai 1 NIV - A Call to Build the House of the LORD - Bible Gateway</u>

To continue our study of Zechariah, Joshua soon helped rebuild the temple In Jerusalem. Haggai and Zechariah used the prophet Joshua to communicate the command to rebuild the temple and encouraged the people as they worked on the wall and the temple. Joshua served as the spiritual leader and high priest who supported the efforts of rebuilding. Joshua was also supported by Zerubbabel, who was the governor of Judea. Joshua was part of the second wave of those returning to Jerusalem to help in the rebuilding of the wall as well as the temple. Remember that just as in Egypt, the children of Israel were also in captivity by the Babylonians. Joshua was probably the first high priest in the newly rebuilt Jerusalem temple and played a significant role in worship.

Joshua appeared before the Throne of God as the high priest with torn and tattered garments. We must look at him as a representation of the Jewish people, dirty and in much distress. The people were full of sin and far away from God because of their sins. This High Priest was dispatched before the Lord with worn and filthy garments to show the sinfulness and the poverty of Israel. They had fallen far from God. So, being far from God, they were very poor, very tattered, very dirty, and full of poverty. There was not much life or cleanliness within the children of Israel as was depicted by the garments worn by Joshua.

This high priest appeared before the throne with the sins of the people represented by the condition of his clothing. He was unfit to be presented to God, as God requires a sacrifice to be without blemish. The service of God could not be conducted in the apparel that Joshua had on. Because he wasn't in the 'proper attire', worship could not take place. God tells u/s to be "holy for I am Holy". There was Satan and his followers reminding God and reminding Joshua that he was not fit for service to God. His sins were too great, as depicted by his condition. We all are in this condition, and those who are wise and humble will realize this. The wise ones realize that their conduct doesn't interest God as much as their Heart.

This was the high priest who was supposed to be a representation of the people of Israel. He had to go before the Holy of Holies and appear before God to pray for and offer sacrifices for God's chosen people so the people could be atoned for their sins. But this Joshua was filthy, dirty, and unsuitable to even be in the presence of God, let alone represent the people that God had chosen. Joshua was reminded of his filthiness by the adversary, Satan himself.

Joshua's condition was a representation of himself as well as the horrible sinfulness of the children of Israel. There is no way that he could represent the children of Israel or even himself before God and be forgiven of his sin. He was standing there alone with no favor, no advocate, and only accusers. Everyone around him saw his condition.

Joshua could not argue that the accusers had a seeing problem or that he was just having a bad day. He did not have any excuse for the sin that was in his life, represented by the filthy clothes. Joshua could not blame society, politics, his mother, his father, his sister, or his brother for the condition that he was in. Joshua also did not separate himself from the sins of the children of Israel. Joshua appeared before the Throne not only with his sins but the sins of the people he represented on his back. There seemed to be no way out of this dilemma. There was nothing there was in Joshua's favored that he could say on his own behalf that would have caused there to be a positive outcome. Joshua was filthy, and the filth represented sin at his uttermost.

The Bible even tells us that the best that we can do is as good as only filthy rags. The image of this filthy rag: it's a worn and muddied piece of cloth that attracts disease-carrying flies. So, Joshua is in dire straits with no way out. The thing to be admired most about Joshua is that even knowing his condition, he still appeared before the Throne of Grace! He still sought mercy before a holy God. He didn't try to hide it and made sure he only came to God after he had gotten "cleaned up," as if that was even possible!

He walked boldly before the Throne of grace, as quoted by the Hebrew writer. He must have wanted to obtain mercy, and this was the **_only_** place that he could obtain mercy. Because Joshua knew his condition, he never said a word. He just walked and presented himself to the Throne. His hope was in the trust he had for this Mighty God. and His lovingkindness. Joshua didn't allow shame and guilt to determine his walk to God's presence. He knew the condition of the people and was carrying the condition of the people of God, as represented by his filthy clothes. Not only was he wearing these filthy garments, he had the adversary, the enemy, reminding him of how bad he was and that he did not deserve to be forgiven of his sins.

My opinion is that is how it is with us today. Many people will not go before the Throne of God because they believe that they do not deserve it or they feel they have nothing to show for it. However, the truth is far from this way of thinking. If we think like this, our meeting with Grace will never occur. I'm here to tell you something. I have learned that love, mercy, and grace are never earned, nor are they ever deserved. James tells us that God resists the proud and would give grace to the humble. It is with humility that we must continually go before the throne of grace to obtain mercy in times of need. We must show up, no matter how filthy we feel. Every day in that time of need!

The rest of the story in Zechariah chapter 3 tells us what happens when you go boldly before the Throne of grace.

The text tells us that Jehovah rebuked Satan, took our side, allowed Grace, Mercy, and Love to do its job, and began to bless and forgive. Unmerited favor blanketed Joshua and his people, not because they deserved or earned it, but because Joshua meant something to God. Because of favor, grace, mercy, and love, Joshua received a change of clothes and new raiment, which represented a new testimony for the people of Israel.

A modern pop-culture reference to the Grace of God can be found in the song Aretha Franklin's Amazing Grace which was a part of a movie of the same name. The lyrics from this classic song say: *Amazing grace, how sweet the sound that saved a wretch like me. I once was lost, but now I'm found, was blind, but now I see.* (AMAZING GRACE - AMAZING GRACE LYRICS (songlyrics.com))

Their sins had been forgiven, and the new clothes represented that God had accepted their worship, humility, and trust in God.

We aren't really that different from Joshua. We are standing before a holy God, filthy dirty, with no way out of sin and nothing to bargain with. We have not gotten to that point where we get to move on from that depiction in our lives. It is not "doom and gloom" but glorious redemption. I think the gospel group The Winans said at best when they said, "what can you know about being restored if he never lost your place?" As Joshua did, the first step for us is to humbly accept our reality. We can never get so busy that we forget and don't have time to make a faith walk boldly before the Throne of Grace.

With all of this new age of living and preaching prosperity, so often we have forgotten the simplicity of the gospel of Christ Jesus. We will always need these words of salvation. We must never forget what it took for God to forgive us. We must go boldly not because we are arrogant, are in the 'right', or have 'moxy' are going to get what a big pot of something. We go boldly because of what the person we know. The person that we know is God, for we know that all things work together for good for those who love the Lord and those who are called for his purpose. We know that it is always better to know than to feel. Many folks will not go before the Lord because of how they 'feel'. By faith, we go before the Lord because of what we KNOW! That grace and mercy is only found at the throne of God.

Sometimes, people tell us that we need to "move on" from the beginning and salvation and go towards prosperity or greater things in life. I'm not sure if we have or need to have that type of mindset. We do have to grow, but we never grow without our foundation of Christ, salvation, and the forgiveness of sin. We have to deal with sins on a daily basis. That's why John 1:9 tells us to confess our sins before God, and he is faithful and just forgives us of our sins and cleanses us of all unrighteousness. John goes on to say that we have Jesus who is our advocate, and he'll never cease to be one. We need an advocate every day, and the day that we don't need one will be the day that we don't need God.

My quest today is to show you how much we need to continue with the simple things of the gospel. The Power of the gospel lies in its simplicity. The gospel tells us that if we confess with our mouths that "the Lord Jesus is our savior and believe in our hearts that he was made to rise from the dead", we shall be saved. The simplicity of the gospel. The Roman writer tells us that nothing shall separate us from the love of God which is Christ Jesus. I think we do need to grow and prosper in Jesus' name. But no matter how much we grow, we will never be above going humbly before the throne to be cleansed by a holy God.

The other thing to point out is God's willingness to forgive us, clean us up, and put us on the right track. God is merciful enough to be willing to look at us through the eyes of the blood of the Lame, which is the blood being stained on every believer by his son Jesus. We need to immerse ourselves in the blood of the Lord. The Bible says that without the shedding of blood, there is no remission or forgiveness of sin. But we do have this life, don't we? Why not make the best of it? Following this is a practical mode of living in day-to-day terms with the sins and the challenges of life. Some of this is therapeutic and mixed in with the spiritualness that is needed for us to succeed.

Reflection Prompts

- What does being "made clean" by God mean to you personally?

- How do you see yourself in the story of Joshua from Zechariah?

- Reflect on a time when you felt unworthy yet experienced grace. What did you learn from it?

- What does salvation mean to you beyond the cross? How does it manifest in your daily life?

CHAPTER: 2
CHOICES

<u>Practical Living And Christianity</u>

This life is often very difficult to live. There's war, grief, and strife all around us. We have become increasingly intolerant towards people who differ from us and only want to be surrounded by those who don't challenge us.s It's gotten even more scary with the introduction of the Internet. These days, folks are attacking and killing each other because of a mere disagreement or call-out on social media. For some reason, we have bought into this sense of 'fairness'. As most of us find out during the course of our lives, and as my mother told me many times, life is not fair. We also know that God is not fair. In the sense that the blessings I get aren't necessarily that you'll be bestowed with. And I'm glad for that fact because the blessings He gives to you, might not interest me. I am more interested in the blessings He gives me! Though not always fair, He is always Just. It doesn't matter what race, religion, creed, background, or sex; God looks at us the same. In my book, there's only one race: the human race. It is we, as humans, that have a problem with folks being different. This idea was born at the Tower of Babel in the bible. We have much in the way of divisions, counterproductive actions, and extremes. And sometimes, the folks creating these divides will claim that they have the "best intentions". This is such a vast subject that it is difficult to make it concise. Let's just say that **our greatest ability, weapon, or tool is the ability to choose**.

We all have choices, and the choices we make determine the life we live. If we choose to rob a bank, we have chosen the consequences that follow. If we choose to be a free, willing participant in sexual activities, we choose the consequences. We don't often think ahead of what the consequences of our choices are. Many folks believe that freedom is the ability to do whatever we want to do because we have the **right** to do it. I don't think this definition does justice to the word freedom. I think freedom also means the responsibility to do what we are 'supposed' to do. It is following the laws, precepts, and moral principles that keep us and our fellow man safe, trusting, and strong. When our nation, or we as individuals, ignore the law, we impact everything around us. That impact is making our surroundings a little unsafe. That's the power of choices.

Then what are we supposed to do? I think we are to choose wisely and hope that's the right choice. Choose based on character, faith, love, and biblical principles, no matter what our vast media audience tells us or says. Our character is what makes us. This is the 'Fruit of the Spirit" (Galatians 5:22-23), which tells us how to practice living. We received these values when we were children and they became solidified around the age of 19-22. We live a life based on these beliefs. Our character and our values are based on what we believe. **_We don't live a life based on what we think; We live a life based on what we believe._** Every day, we have the ability to choose these character and valued traits that we will practice. We often get in trouble and become anxious, depressed, lonely, and angry when we compromise these beliefs or allow these character beliefs to be violated and choose others that are the opposite of our values. Having sex with someone because everyone thinks you should is a compromise of your values, isn't it? Lying to your girlfriend just to stay 'out of trouble' is a compromise of your values. If doing illicit drugs goes against your character and values and you do them out of peer pressure, then you know something is wrong. You will realize that when you align your life to your values, you tend to live a life with more stability. Once your life is stable, the level of anxiety and depression appear not to be as intense.

When we allow our values to be compromised or violated, we, by definition, become angry. This doesn't justify hurting others or other people's property. We may get angry when someone is driving erratically. We may become angry when the lyrics of a song put women down with degrading language. All these instances violate our character, our worth, and our beliefs about ourselves.

What are some examples of our Core Character beliefs? Some positive examples include believing that we are **Courageous, Honest, Trustworthy, Determined, Loyal, Loving, Caring, Strong, Organized, Kind, Patience, Family man/Family woman, Faithful, etc.**

Let's use the character trait of Courageous. To me, being courageous is ***doing your best and standing on your truthful values, even though you are scared out of your mind***. It takes courage to be the only one who doesn't go the way of your "so-called" friends or peers. It takes courage to say no to a boss who tries to get you involved in unfair practices. It is an act of courage to keep living instead of attempting to harm or kill yourself. It takes courage to ask for help. Courage is a big word and a mighty item to use as our strength. God told Joshua to be Strong and Courageous, which is an example of a character trait that, if we live by, will cause us to be stable. **We are not courageous because we do courageous things; We do courageous things because we are courageous.** Our character isn't wholly based on what we do but is innate within us based on what we were taught, what we learned, and our life experiences. So, all of us go through life choosing the character traits we want for us as well as the things in life that we're willing to compromise. Woe unto those who settle down to doing the opposite of our strength, our values, and our character. When there is no resistance, the 'other guy', the opposite of our strengths, will win. That 'other guy' takes the shape of beliefs like **Can't Get It Right, Guilty, Not Good Enough, Unlovable, Never Safe, Can't Trust, Why Me, Abandoned, Alone.** There are more items we can add to this list. Often folks believe that they are what they 'feel'. If you feel like an idiot, it must mean you are an idiot. If you feel angry, it must mean you've been mistreated. If you feel scared, you must be in danger. And this list goes on. Choosing to live life by how you feel can be problematic. **Our feelings were never created to be our decision-makers.** Our feelings are there to respond/react to daily items that happen to us in the present. The Latin word for emotion, emotere, literally means "energy in motion". Our emotions are only there to be felt as sensations of energy moving through the body, such as tension or expansion. They are fluid resources that should be felt and released, not repressed or ruminated upon. When we reminisce on our past, it can illicit feelings, but they bring feelings that were already experienced at the time of that event. In other words, when we feel it is because of something that JUST happened. When we bring the past or future in as a focus and attach them to the feelings, we may intensify or extend anger, anxiety, and depression for longer than we need to.

Fear is another big item that is part of the 'other guy' list. The Bible tells us that God has not given us the spirit of fear but of love, power, and a sound mind. Technically, fear is not a feeling. Fear is a belief system. The belief is that hurt and pain are near, and we have to guard against it, even if that 'thing' isn't there. When we walk in that life based on fear, we can count on making terrible decisions. Can you imagine always walking around in fear of something bad happening to you? Can you imagine how stressful it can be to consider everything around you as a threat? Constant fear can lead to living in constant flight or fight mode, which increases the production of the stress hormone cortisol. Excess cortisol causes its own host of problems, such as weight gain, bad skin, inflammation, and mood swings.

If you keep living this way, then when do you get to enjoy life? When do you get to be happy, and when do you get to be at peace? When do you just relax and get to hang out with your loved ones? I believe that this is what often keeps folks who have experienced traumatic events from enjoying life. Past trauma keeps them on guard, and their brain convinces them that danger is ever-present. However, there's good news: making choices does not require feelings, just the knowledge of our positive character that is based on godly morals and our beliefs. Romans tells us: "And we know that all things work together for good to them who love the Lord and to the called according to His purpose." We simply have to know our choices. We do not have to 'feel' in order to choose. Our feelings have a purpose, but they must not be what we rely on to make an informed decision. Our brain was created for that. It is ok to have fun and enjoy life. All of those things happen at the moment: enjoying life, having fun, etc.

David said in the Psalms: *Though I walk through the valley of the shadow of death, I will fear no evil for thou are with me.* Something interesting about what David said is that there is a shadow. Shadows only occur when there's light. We must remember that there has been and always will be light. Here, David was referring to the light of God in his life, which is ever-present. You always have character traits to choose from. And there's never a day that this choice is not yours to own and practice.

The 'other guy' wants you to believe that you don't have any choices. The 'other guy' wants you to believe that you must concede to defeat, and this other way of living is to compromise your values. This leads to anxiety, depression, loneliness, resentment, self-pity, and self-harm. Betraying your values and then going through so many negative emotions is no way to live. The more choices you have, the better able you are to handle life's anxiety-filled situations. Feeling like we don't have many choices can lead to a feeling of helplessness and make our anxiety more intense. We need to recognize that our ability to choose may be our greatest weapon and one of our greatest character traits. Choose wisely based on who you are and not how others have labeled you.

Reflection Prompts

- Bring to mind a time when you did something that goes against your values. Journal about how that made you feel and if it led to resentment in the future.

- Reflect on a time when living out your values brought joy or clarity.

CHAPTER: 3

FOCUS

Practical Living And Christianity

The world is full of things that are trying to divert our focus from what's important. Especially in today's age, we're in a continuous battle against all the distractions that surround us. For example, when we are walking across the street, and we hear a car horn, see a bird flying from one tree to another, or see a billboard ad, our thoughts immediately turn toward that direction. There are always things that will attract our attention to them. These things often change our thoughts, our emotions, and the direction we walk in life. Think about being late for an appointment and being stopped at a traffic light. In the car next to you, the person has a big dog with his head stuck out of the window doing something funny. You forget about being late for those few minutes and start to chuckle at the dog. We have so many gadgets in our society that take away our attention and focus. There seems to always be the 'next big thing' in the world that we must consume or buy. The latest iPhone, the latest coffee drink, the latest this and that. That's why marketing is so popular these days. The commercials we're constantly seeing are the product of a brand's marketing campaigns. And these commercials are trying to convince us that we must get **this** gadget or thing…NOW!

Our want or desire to have this stuff often changes our focus and our direction from what's essential to our core self. Let's consider a personal anecdote here. I grew up in the countryside. We used to drink grape sodas and eat sardines and crackers in the cotton fields in Alabama. There was one particular thing that I always loved to eat as a boy: banana flips! These were so very good, sweet, and…WOW! They don't make those anymore. The other day, I was thinking about a banana flip. The thoughts occupied my mind, and soon, I'd started an internet search. I searched and browsed multiple sites looking for this childhood treat. Before I knew it, a couple of hours had passed.

Did you see how my focus and my direction were changed by wanting a banana flip?

Our focus will determine the direction we walk and the ground on which we stand. Often, things come up in our lives that will blur our focused vision. The loss of someone close, without question, will divert our focus. Grief may lead us to think about the memories we had with them on a loop. We will focus on the hurt and pain that this loss has caused us. This hurt and pain, quite naturally, is our focus. It drains us and becomes our life for a time. Some folks have been traumatized in many different forms, and trauma has the same effect on us. For instance, when someone is sexually abused, even as an adult, it completely changes the focus and direction of their lives. These events are usually of a life-threatening and harmful nature and usually out of the victim's control. This trauma rewires the person's brain chemistry and changes their perception of self. These people then start to associate different labels with themselves, which eventually become their core beliefs or feelings that are always lingering. We'll refer to these labels as names here. For example, we who have experienced sexual, physical, or emotional trauma as a child might give themselves these labels because of the traumatic experiences.

Some of the names are Not Good Enough, My Fault, Why Me, Failure, Guilty, Never Safe, Not Strong Enough, Weak, Unlovable, Bad Guy, Unworthy, etc. These are called **Negative Core Beliefs**. Our self-worth can become affected/changed based on the beliefs that these life experiences have taught us. People with trauma can develop a more narrowed way of thinking, and their trauma may center the age of their focus. Triggers in life, such as smells, sounds, noise, anniversaries, holidays, and events, can cause a remembrance of these focus names/labels. Experiencing things like depression, anxiety, sadness, loneliness, irritability, frustration, and guilt can also point this person toward the focus of the names that the trauma gave them. Their ability to have an imagination or to create something different in their life becomes compromised. They are stuck in this focus. Until there is a change, this is their focus: those names. Sadly, as the famous author Emily Blunt said once, **"None of us escape life unscathed."** Most of us experience some trials and tribulations in our lives and they can cause us to lose focus. Look at Peter and his focus while he walks on water.

Jesus Walks on the Water Matthew 14:22-32 (NIV)

[22] Immediately Jesus made the disciples get into the boat and go on ahead of him to the other side, while he dismissed the crowd. [23] After he had dismissed them, He went up on a mountainside by himself to pray. Later that night, he was there alone, [24] and the boat was already a considerable distance from land, buffeted by the waves because the wind was against it.

[25] Shortly before dawn, Jesus Went out to them, walking on the lake. [26] When the disciples saw him walking on the lake, they Were terrified. "It's a ghost," they said and cried out in fear.

[27] But Jesus immediately said to them: "Take courage! It is I. Don't be afraid."

[28] "Lord, if it's you," Peter replied, "tell me to come to you on the water."

[29] "Come," he said.
Then Peter got down out of the boat, walked on the water and came toward Jesus. [30] But when he saw the wind, he was afraid and, beginning to sink, cried out, "Lord, save me!"

[31] Immediately Jesus reached out his hand and caught him. "You of little faith," he said, "why did you doubt?"

[32] And when they climbed into the boat, the wind died down. [33] Then those who were in the boat worshiped him, saying, "Truly you are the Son of God."

Peter realized that he could not walk on water but wanted to be close to Jesus. He was afraid and lacked courage. And that's why Jesus told them not to be afraid and to have courage. Isn't that what Jesus is telling us today when faced with great odds in our lives? Isn't that what Jesus is telling us when those always unexpected events rock our lives? Isn't that what Jesus is telling us when we are going through those difficult times? Jesus was near the disciples, and they were still afraid and without courage. If we consider ourselves Jesus's disciples, then we will always have him near us, even when the waters are raging and beyond our control. Even when we don't see the end, He is there. Even when all seems lost, He is there. Even when the way out seems distant, He is right there telling us that we should not fear and to be of good courage.

Peter wanted to get to Jesus but needed one thing to do that — **FAITH**. He had to, somehow, trust Jesus. He had to go to Jesus with faith in order to get there. And we're not so different from Peter. When we are faced with things in our life, all we need is faith. Even though the waters were raging, Jesus was still on solid ground. He was standing in the same place where the disciples could not stand. This story compels us to the truth that all things are possible with God.

However, if our focus is on the trauma, the junk, and the mess, the ground under our feet can become shaky and unsustainable. Peter walked out with one step, with faith. He put the other foot out. It is indicated here that as long as Peter's focus was on Jesus, he was walking on unstable ground.

Who else can actually walk on water? Water is not something that is meant for walking. Water is meant for drinking, cooking, bathing and other such uses. But Jesus was walking on water, and so was Peter. Jesus is walking on solid ground, and so is Peter. Peter discovered that as long as his focus was on Jesus, his ground was solid, and his direction was clear. Therefore, as long as we focus on Jesus, our ground will be solid, and our direction will be clear.

As soon as Peter lost his focus, the realities of his frailties affected his view of life at that moment. The situation became bigger than him, and he allowed his focus to turn to himself and his inability to control. Fear and doubt crept into Peter's mind as he realized the extremity of the task. Our focus on things like our character traits, the godly fruit of the spirit, can help us in our decision-making.

Philippians 4:6-7 tells us:

> [6] Do not be anxious about anything, but in every situation, by prayer and petition, with thanksgiving, present your requests to God. [7] And the peace of God, which transcends all understanding, will guard your hearts and your minds in Christ Jesus.

(bible gateway https://www.biblegateway.com)

The Bible doesn't direct us towards anything that we're already doing of our own will. That being said, I think we can't really avoid worrying about things in life. Our worries signify that we care about something and prompt us to action. But for clarity purposes, this text is referring to undue worry about circumstances. It is a focus that causes us to hold on to that "thing" longer than necessary and with such a tight grip that we become consumed. We care about jobs, money, our mates, our children, our health, and so many other things. Undue worry creeps in and turns our care into an obsession about what can go wrong. Sometimes, The thing about worry is that it also gives us a chance to choose what to focus on and determine the direction we walk in. For instance, if we focus on the issues or the problems and look at them as the source of defining us today, they will surely define us. This means that there is another choice. This is what David said about focus in **Psalm 121:**

I will lift up mine eyes unto the hills, from whence cometh my help.

[2] My help cometh from the LORD, which made heaven and earth.

³ He will not suffer thy foot to be moved: he that keepeth thee will not slumber.

⁴ Behold, he that keepeth Israel shall neither slumber nor sleep.

⁵ The LORD is thy keeper: the LORD is thy shade upon thy right hand.

⁶ The sun shall not smite thee by day, nor the moon by night.

⁷ The LORD shall preserve thee from all evil: he shall preserve thy soul.

⁸ The LORD shall preserve thy going out and thy coming in from this time forth, and even for evermore.

King James Version (KJV)

(bible gateway https://www.biblegateway.com)

We can have worry and anxiety and can still focus on what gives us strength. We can focus on our Maker and Sustainer, who provides us strength. Our strength doesn't come from the things that bring us distress or pull us down but from the **One** who is always there to lift us up.

Reflection Prompts:

- Reflect on a time when losing focus led you astray. What helped you regain direction?

- Write about a "shadow" in your life. How can you embrace the light and move forward?

CHAPTER: 4

ILLUSION OF CONTROL

Often, we believe that the situations have control over us because it is validated or made real by our focus. There are a couple of things that validate the situation as having control over us to cause us to lose our focus:

I.   **Our Emotions**: Worry, anxiety, fear, anger, frustration, and depression are just a few of the emotions that all humans face. In and of themselves, these are natural reactions to things that we all experience. The reason that I say this is because emotions are innate to being human, and none of us can escape that reality. However, our focus will determine the frequency, duration, and intensity of the emotions. It is quite common for us to make decisions based on our emotions. But that doesn't make it the right or healthy thing to do. Please remember: Our emotions were never created to be our decision-makers. It is easy to get carried on the wave of emotions we're feeling at the time and make rash decisions. Just because they feel *this* way, it seems that their behavior or actions is justified. Our feeling often gives us a reason to go in 'that' direction in life. Just think how many everyday decisions you make under the influence of your emotions. You may feel attracted to someone and decide that they'll be your partner or soulmate. People go out and buy expensive and long-term assets just because they feel like it. We might even be conditioned to eat something unhealthy if we're feeling a certain way, such as upset or out of control.

People decide to commit suicide and don't realize that the emotions they're feeling during that time will surely pass. People might even break up or get a divorce from their partner because they felt angry with them and thought that feeling would stay forever. Many folks say rash and hurtful things based on how they feel at the time. Look at what our Brother Paul says about focus and how we should walk in 2 Corinthians 5:7: For We walk by faith, not by sight. It is very important to note also that none of the Fruit of the Spirit is an emotion. Galatians 5:22-23: **But the fruit of the Spirit is love, joy, peace, longsuffering, gentleness, goodness, faith, Meekness, temperance: against such there is no law**. And in Ephesians 5:9: *For the fruit of the Spirit is in all goodness and righteousness and truth;)*.

II. **Our Labels**: The other items that cause us to lose our focus are the labels we use. Our words can reaffirm the belief that a particular situation has control over us. These words are: Shoulda, Woulda, Coulda, Wish, If, Might, Maybe, Always, Never, Can't Don't, Won't. These are self-defeating words. They divert focus to the past, black-and-white thinking, and the future. This language leads us to lament the past and worry about controlling the future. These words attempt to change an outcome. What happens in a marriage when someone says, "I knew I shoulda listened to mama and not marry you!" This statement is based on a wish to change the outcome. That person may not like what their mate is doing right now, and they foolishly believe that they 'should've' seen it when they first got married. This thought/belief is crazy! We only know what we know at the time, and we do our best to use it. Life only grants us that unique knowledge through our experience. I often wish I knew 'then' what I know 'now'. But don't we all? These extreme words help us to focus on things we can't control or ever change. This is the classic definition of stress: **An attempt to control something you can't or was never meant to**. You got your guy now; deal with it! Mama didn't even know about him then.

III. **Interpretative Language**: Our language, or self-talk, determines many things about us. Our language determines what we like, where we go, the decisions we make, the partners we choose, and what we will or won't allow in our lives. We make decisions about our self-worth based on what we tell ourselves. When you were young, your parents may have instilled many things in your personality and life. These things, as you grow older, show up in your regular life and influence your decision-making. Sometimes, negative events, such as betrayal, abandonment, or trauma, happen to you when you are young and vulnerable. All of these things can alter your view of life, trust, and relationships. Gabor Mate is an addiction expert, speaker, and author who says that trauma is not what happened to us; it's what happens inside you as a result of what happened to you." It's also important how we make sense of what happens to us in our lives and language is our best bet to accomplish that well.

The language we have is often based on our beliefs about ourselves. If we believe we are '**Not good enough**,' this is how we will walk in life, and this is the language that we will use to keep reaffirming the belief. What we continuously think eventually turns into a core belief. I'd like to remind you that we don't live a life based on what we think; we live a life based on what we believe. If our internal monologue tells us that we are a 'monster', our language will dictate this. This language, in turn, will cause an emotional reaction such as anxiety, sadness, anger, etc. The language with which we interpret our experiences can intensify emotional reactions. If someone believes that they are not safe, their language will do its best to ensure that their belief is somehow believable. However, being believable is not the same as being true. We even make a lie believable if we twist our words enough.

Interpretative Language means the words with which we interpret something. It's a concept that says that often, the language that we hear in the present doesn't fit what we want to hear, or it doesn't sound familiar to us. Therefore, our mind will add things to it so our language has a different and negative meaning. Our negative experiences from the past can affect what words and language we use in the present. The statements may have been true in the past but are more than likely not be true now. When we add the past to what is happening in the present it often comes with a labeling of the situation or person. This is often tough because the past has already happened.

We may say things like, "I know what you meant!" "You always do that". Another interpretive language phrase is the statement, 'I feel like…" which is not a feeling but a thought or belief. Feelings are items like Anger, Anxiety, Happy, Sad, etc. We can't feel 'like'. The 'feel like, seem like, or look like' statements can often 'justify' what is said as being 'valid' and not to be questioned. 'I feel like you don't love me.' "Looks like you are interested in that girl over there." "Seems like I'm not important to you anymore." Where is the evidence that indicates that these conclusory statements are true? Usually, the statements are based on 'feeling' of anger, fearfulness, confusion, or anxiety that the past has already defined as being threatening. This language is quite powerful and can stir internal chaos in individuals and disruption in relationships. This language is based solely on a one-sided interpretation of what is said or done in the present. This type of language doesn't take into consideration that the other person had a different intention or meaning behind the action, decision, or communication. The conclusion of what happened has already been made with little chance of it changing by the person using this language.

When interpretative language happens in a relationship, the mate will more than likely react in kind. When our language is based on an interpretative viewpoint, it skews our view and causes us to interpret most language as an attack, a put-down, or something negative. This can bring about a lot of resentment between two people. This language may indicate that the spouse doesn't care and is on the warpath. The conflict may ensue, and many times, a 'winner' has to be declared. This means finding a place to get hurtful, painful language. There are no bigger weapons than the ones that have already worked: THE PAST! There are all sorts of language, words, name-calling, labels, and failures that can be found in the past. And people know that language works because it worked in the past. The historical language reminds that person how they never got it right, how small they are, how there is always somebody better, and how they miss the mark. We or their partner does something positive, and the other attacks with a non-response or a defensive response. This comes from the negative meanings we assign to language that often makes the 'attack' more intense and guarantees distance, questioning of trust, and living in insecurity.

This negative language can also be self-attacking. The feelings may indicate that something is 'wrong' because the feeling is present. Often, feelings come 'pre-defined' based on life experiences. For example, many people have already defined anxiety as the following: Not safe, something bad is about to happen, I have to get out of here, I'm bad again, got to get rid of this feeling. These are 'horrible' definitions for anxiety. If this is the definition we use for anxiety, their view of their world will always be tainted.

For example, often, what keeps someone from having a good night's sleep can be the self-talk that person has when they lay their heads down. Where does the person's mind go? To the past? To the mistakes they believe they made during the day? Does it go to what they may have labeled as missed opportunities? Maybe that significant other said something that has that person riled up. This language may also cause someone to make bad in life. For example, if we have had some past negative life experiences, it has already 'tainted' our view of the world, trust, and ourselves.

Jumping to conclusions comes to mind during this Interpretative Language. Jumping to Conclusions is a sort of cognitive distortion. It's a way of thinking that says I can predict things and make assumptions about the future even though I have limited information and evidence. I can label you like I want to even if I know it's not true. "I know you meant to hurt me (even if you didn't), and even if I have no evidence to prove it." **Jumping to conclusions** is an obstacle to communication, where we make judgments or even decide the outcome without having all the facts or any evidence to reach a truthful conclusion. For example, when someone is jumping to conclusions, they might assume that someone they just met is angry at them. They assumed this simply because that person wasn't smiling at them while they talked, even though there are many other alternative explanations for that behavior.

Mind-reading is another cognitive distortion that says: I know what you are thinking without there being any evidence of it. I don't know what I'm thinking half the time, and you have some superpower that gives you the ability to read my mind? If you know what I'm thinking, please let me know, too! Maybe you should quit your job, get a 1-900 number, and advertise how you can read minds. All jokes aside, we can never know what the other person was or is thinking unless they communicate about it. Don't you think this sounds a little familiar to fortune's telling? Saying that I have the power to predict the future sounds foolish. It's somewhat like saying: "If you do X, then Y is going to happen." Unless you're a mathematician, the chances of your hypothesis being right are very low.

This Interpretative Language causes us to lose our focus. We forget that we are fighting someone that we cherish, that we love, that we have children with. Why are we at war with someone who shares our bed, our food, and our hearts? We have to forget all these facts if we are to fight with this much ferocity.

Our language has a big role to play in how our mood will be, our emotions will be and what decisions we make. Take some time to reflect on the following:

- What are you telling yourself when you are tempted?

- What are you saying when things don't go your way?

- What is the language you use when you go through trials?

- What is your first move when you believe we have been mistreated?

Writing down the answers to the above questions can point out major themes of the language you use. Being aware of how we speak about others and ourselves is the first step to changing it.

Our language determines a lot about how strong and secure we feel. We are not referring to toxic positivity or empty positive quotes, though affirmations have been known to shift things. The human experience is never 100% positive. You need to be able to tell the truth and accept the reality, even when it's not positive! All that truth is a "restatement of FACTS". Hence, truth cannot differ from one person to another. When that happens, it's mostly the truth being confused with opinions. An opinion is when we both look at the same thing and see something different. The truth is one thing. Tell the truth about you and your character. Tell the truth about what is happening so that you can actually hear it. Tell the truth about the reality of your situation. Often, we do not tell the truth about what is happening. Our language might be reaffirming what has already happened and not describing what's happening currently. Our brains try to convince us that since it happened last time, it is probably going to happen again.

So, what is the point I'm trying to make? All our emotions are ok to be experienced and a natural part of life. However, rather than feelings, our faith, the decisions we make, and our truthful character should determine our focus. Initially, our emotions are always about what we JUST experienced. Our emotions only get out of control, become intense, and last a long time when we leave the right now and bring the past and future into the picture.

Reflection Prompts:

• Write about a belief or label you've carried from the past. How can you rewrite that narrative?

CHAPTER:5

REDIRECTING TO THE PRESENT

There is a term or concept called Grounding or Mindfulness. They help us to stay present in the current moment or where our feet are planted by using our five senses. There's no better place to make a decision than the present. In fact, that is the ONLY place you can make a decision. You can't make a decision yesterday, nor can you make a decision tomorrow. You can plan for the future or reminisce about the past. But, when it comes to decisions, the ones in the past have already been made, and you don't know what the future will bring, so you can't make a decision yet.

Often, due to negative life experiences, we tend to focus on either Old or Futuristic things in our lives. Both of these can cause instability when they become our focus. Many people, when they deem a situation as "heavy" or "emotional", have an automatic process of associating it with what happened in their past. Below is a chart of the struggle with our past or future being our focus:

Historic Focus		Futuristic Focus
Causes Instability		Causes Instability
Reason:1. We typically reinterpret the past or add things that never happened.		Reason: We're trying to gain a sense of control by focusing on the Future.
2. We make attempts to change the past.		The two things we attempt to control: 1. People 2. Events
2a. When we use words like shoulda, If, woulda, coulda, wish, might, maybe, and ought to, it is an attempt to change the outcome of our past.		
Fear dominates the person. This can interfere with choices.		Fear dominates the person,which interferes with choices.

Historic: There can be a constant need to get rid of our past by changing the outcome. When a friend of mine decided to go a different way home, he ran into a huge traffic stop due to an accident. The first thing he said was: "I *shoulda* went the other way!" He said this based on an outcome that he didn't know about at the time he made the decision to go the other way home. I think we do this with our past. We look back over those items when we are feeling anxious, angry, or depressed, and we add things that *never* happened at the time the event happened. We say things like.

"I shoulda left him years ago."

"I wish I had never gone to that party because that's where I was assaulted."

"If I had just listened, then this stuff would not have happened."

"I shoulda told him how I really felt".

What we forget is that at the time we made those decisions, we didn't know what we knew after the event happened. We know a whole lot more now than we did at the time the event happened. **We can only know what we know at the time, and we often forget this because of what we know now.** At the time of the decision we could not have known what was actually going to happen. People often say, "I knew that was going to happen." Well, I beg the differ. I think that if we actually knew, we would have made a different decision. The silly thing about attempts to change the outcome of our past is that, deep down, we know it's not possible. That's the instability part when we attempt to change something that we can't, leading to frustration and stress. Stress kills joy and keeps fear alive. My definition of fear is "*anticipating hurt and pain*". We fear things and deem them as a threat because that's how we interpret them. It's different for everybody. I don't necessarily mean phobias. People may fear getting into a relationship based solely on hurt from previous relationships. The relationship that person is in now is a different relationship. Often, we all fall into the same relational dynamics because we're used to them or because they feel familiar. We keep choosing the same 'type' of person and expecting different results. If that is the case, such as choosing an abuser, we should anticipate a similar outcome. That withstanding, new experiences will always be somewhat different. Anxiety often accompanies things in our life that are New and Different. That is a pretty *normal* response.

Every time we revisit our past, we find that nothing has changed, and we get triggered the same. We can never go back and erase the horrific or terrifying things that happened. A certain memory or event will always be at the time and date it originally happened. However, what we can do is not let the past muddle our present relationships, decisions, and actions. Sadly, couples often fall victim to this phenomenon. Both partners use their past hurts and pains as weapons to ward off the other person because of their fear and insecurities. So many couples fight, and the fight intensifies when one or the other (or both) bring up the past misbehaviors of their mate. If someone cheated in their past, it will continue to be an irreversible part of their history. When your partner reminds you that you left him and were gone for a month, it means that their mind still has a clear picture of that event. If we constantly bring up past events and use them as weapons, we remind the other person that they can never change what they did or themselves. We tell them that they now represent hurt and pain no matter what they do. Usually, someone brings up the past of the other to justify their anger and their discomfort. Once we're in an emotionally triggered state, it feels nice to stay there. And to intensify and escalate emotional responses, we have to use the past hurts and pains of our past to put the 'fuel on the fire'.

Bitterness, frustration, and anger will grow the more you feed into them. Whenever I come across a bitter person, my first thought is that this is someone who is walking around with unforgiveness. Forgiveness is the most appropriate response to previous hurts and pains. Forgiving others and yourself is essential for healthy relationships as well as a healthy focus on the present. Note that forgiveness doesn't necessarily mean that you 'forget', 'feel better', 'are ok with what happened', 'let it go', or 'got over it'. On the contrary, *I believe that forgiveness is defined as a decision made. It's a choice of how you are going to treat the person who wronged you. You must not reduce them to that 'thing' they did to you.* In that decision of forgiveness, it also means that the past will not be weaponized to hurt the other person. If a good friend came to your house and 'accidentally' stole something, the resentful part who doesn't want to forgive would want to treat them like a thief. When they call you, you might answer, "Hello, thief. So, who did you rob today"? The friend would be harshly reminded through your treatment that you haven't forgiven them.

Jesus told Peter that he would deny him three times before the rooster crowed during his movement from judgment hall to judgment hall on the days leading up to his crucifixion. Of course, Peter didn't accept that he would deny Christ. Just as Jesus predicted, Peter denied Jesus three times. When Jesus came back after his resurrection to the upper room, he met with Peter by asking Peter three times, "Do you love me? Feed my lambs". This happened three times, signifying the three times of denial. The purpose of what Jesus did was to restore the relationship. It was to ensure that the fellowship between him and Peter was still strong. When it comes to **forgiveness**, the goal has to be to ensure that the relationship is restored and its strength is still intact. This principle goes for a wife, husband, friend, family member, children, extended family, coworker, and most importantly *YOURSELF*.

Futuristic: The need to control is powerful. I do not mean 'controlling' in the general sense. We are talking about the concept of control in terms of trauma. The two criteria for an event being traumatic are: 1. The event is uncontrollable. 2. The event is unexpected. These two criteria are what make an event traumatic. For example, 911 in New York was unexpected and uncontrollable. Someone being raped or assaulted is unexpected and uncontrollable.

Being T-Boned in an intersection is unexpected and uncontrollable. A traumatic event is also defined as one 1) that poses a threat of serious injury or death to oneself or others and 2) elicits feelings of intense fear, helplessness, or horror. Since these are the criteria for an event being traumatic, the person who experienced the event constantly attempts to ensure that that thing never happens again. Hence, they believe that controlling people and events can keep them safe. The need to control results in a constant 'stress-fest'. Again, a reasonable or non-traumatized person knows that they cannot control the future, but that doesn't stop many people from attempting to. Because of this need to control, they never believe they are safe. Safety is always a perception and not always a reality. We are only as safe as we believe ourselves to be. For example, we all grow up in different kinds of environments and around different sorts of people. You and your friends likely have a different meaning for the word safe, depending on your upbringing. A neighborhood you consider safe may feel extremely dangerous to your friend.

There is a better way of looking at our lives than what we're used to, and the chart below outlines it.

Historic Focus	Here and Now Focus	Futuristic Focus
Causes Instability	Causes Stability	Causes Instability
Reason:1.We typically reinterpret the past	Reason: 1. This is where your feet are planted 2. This is the only place where *decisions* can be made	Reason: We need a lot of control when our focus is on the Future
2. We make attempts to change the past	3. This is the only place where **Love** can be demonstrated	The two things we attempt to control: 1. People 2. Events
2a. We use words like shoulda, If, woulda, coulda, wish, might, maybe, and ought to that is an attempt to change the outcome of our past	4. This is the only place where **Trust** can be experienced	The extreme words appear in their focus: Always, Never, can't ever, Have to, Don't, Must, Won't
Fear dominates the person, which interferes with choices.	Safety Dominates	Fear dominates the person, which interferes with choices.

God is a right-now God. When God moves, He moves right now. When He blesses us, it's right now. When He does what He does, He does it in the present. That's why we can always say that He has done great things. When our focus is on the present, the here and now, we are much more stable. It is right now that's happening at the moment. You can only love someone in the moment that you have. We must agree that since love is a verb, it requires action. The action or demonstration of love has to happen in the present with genuine intent. We can't love anyone yesterday or tomorrow. We only have it right now. We can only make a decision in the present. We can't make a decision yesterday or tomorrow.

Now is the only time we have to make a choice. We may regret a choice we have made, but the time to make it has already passed, and it's fixed now. We may want to make a decision tomorrow, but we have to wait until tomorrow becomes today in order to make that decision. It is having your feet planted in the now that keeps us grounded. You need to realize that you can be stable even when things are tough in your life. It is in the present decision to choose that materializes our strength. Putting on the whole armor of God is a present-time decision.

The late great Inez Andrews said it best in her song: ***Lord Don't Move My Mountain***.

> Now, Lord, don't move my mountain,
> But give me the strength to climb,
> And Lord, don't take away my stumbling blocks,
> But lead me all around.

https://www.google.com/search?q=inez+andrews+lord+don%27t+move+that+mountain

That's in the 'now'. Many folks who have had a series of negative life events or trauma find it difficult to focus on the 'here and now' because their past dominates their thoughts. Their past is always in their mind's driver's seat, attempting to change the outcome or control the future so the same things don't hurt them again. I'm here to tell you that the present is the best and safest place to be. It is the place where God moves, strengthens, speaks to us, and grows us.

Reflection Prompts

- Reflect on a time when forgiveness was difficult. What steps helped you let go at that time?

- How does understanding God's forgiveness influence the way you forgive others?

CHAPTER: 6

LOVE AND RELATIONSHIPS

We humans have an innate need to be loved. Research suggests that babies can actually die from a lack of physical touch or affection. So it makes sense why we all yearn for a friend, family member, or romantic partner in our lives. Most of us have been fed the concept of love through pop culture, music, movies, and books. I regret to report that all of these depictions of love are misleading and lead to more heartbreak. No human can meet the expectations we have formed due to the popular definitions of love.

Moreover, dysfunctional families, romantic disappointments, betrayals, abandonments, and other tragic things can often interfere with our belief that we're all innately loveable. Complex trauma or other tragic life events can often lead us to believe that we are 'unlovable'. We can often believe that no one will ever love us because of our past. The belief that we have too much 'baggage' starts sounding real. The 'unforgivable' word seems to loom large.

Love is such an important part of recovery from trauma, anxiety, depression, and other relational issues. Let's define love. We will not use what the dictionary tells us because it involves 'feelings'. Love is not a feeling. In my book, love is a decision and a choice. This choice is based on our character, values, and beliefs. Our feelings were never created to be our decision-makers; our brains were. The choice to love is made based on our love needs and character. I also think *love is intentional, focused, and has a lot of energy*. This saying indicates, especially in a marital relationship, that this is micro, laser-focused with the goal of hitting the target with the result of causing our mate to be convinced that they are valued, cherished and important to you in a moment.

There is a book called *The 5 Love Languages* by Gary Chapman that outlines different ways that people express love and want to be loved in return. Everything about love is giving and surrendering. When the focus is on receiving, it is no longer love. Love is a verb which means it requires action. Love is not love unless it is demonstrated. Romans 5:6-8 tells us:

6 For when We Were yet without strength, in due time, Christ died for the ungodly.

7 For scarcely for a righteous man will one die: yet peradventure for a good man some would even dare to die.

8 But God commendeth (demonstrated*) his love toward us, in that, while We Were yet sinners, Christ died for us.*

It is not just in the efforts; it is focused efforts that make you and others feel loved in the way they need. When I was in the military, we used to go to the range to 'qualify' our weapon, such as an M16. If we were deployed, we would take that weapon with us. So, we had to qualify with this weapon to ensure that it performed as required. At the range, there were pop-up silhouettes that we had to knock down. We had to knock down a required amount to be qualified with our weapon. There were the 50 meters, 100 meters, 150 meters, 200 meters, 250 meters, and 300 meters. I used to hate the 300-meter one because I could never hit it! If you didn't knock down the required number of targets, you had to go to the back of the line to be 'retrained' by an expert. He would help you recalibrate your weapon. But no matter how much you recalibrated your weapon, it never affected the **velocity** of the round. The velocity is our 'trying', which often gets mistaken for results.

The trying, when applied to wanting to love another person, may not be the issue. The goal is to hit the required number of targets to qualify. With our mates and with people we care about, we have to 'learn' how to 'hit the target' more and more often. In essence, we need to learn how the other person is loved and what makes them feel cherished and valued. This is purposeful. I think that is what gets us in trouble when it comes to love; our focus is on what we can get rather than what we can give. Learning to do this does take much in the way of trust. Trust and love are like twins; it's extremely tough to have one without the other. Trust is not trust unless it is experienced. And the experience of trust comes in the moment. For instance, you ask someone to do something for or with you. When this person does that thing with or for you, you just experience trust with/from them.

Another issue in this realm is that a lot of us only love people based on how we want to be loved. We do not love others based on how they want to be loved because we typically don't know how. People often receive love differently. One person may like to cuddle and like the touch of their mate, but their mate may like to just spend some quality time together. Others may like to receive encouraging words or affirming words. Some like to receive small sentimental gifts, while others receive love through varying acts of service. The key is to LEARN how to love each other in a way that is focused, intentional, and enthusiastic so as to cause the other person to be convinced that they are cherished, valuable, and cared about. Of course, this happens at the moment. Love is exercised and demonstrated in the moments that you have. You cannot love anyone yesterday, and you cannot love anyone tomorrow. Loved is demonstrated in that very moment that you have. The intent comes in the moment, the focus comes in the moment, and the energy is in that very moment.

The question may not be *if* you love someone. The question may be **_how_** to love someone.

Focus on the family does a great job of explaining the aspects of the 5 Love Languages. Below is the excerpt:

Words of affirmation

One way to express love emotionally is to use words that build up. Solomon, author of ancient Hebrew Wisdom Literature, wrote, "The tongue has the power of life and death" (Proverbs 18:21, NIV). Many couples have never learned the tremendous power of verbally affirming each other.

Verbal compliments, or words of appreciation, are powerful communicators of love. They are best expressed in simple, straightforward statements of affirmation, such as:

"You look sharp in that suit."

"Don't you look incredible in that dress?! Wow!"

"I really like how you're always on time to pick me up at work."

"You can always make me laugh."

Words of <u>affirmation</u> are one of the five basic love languages. Within that language, however, there are many dialects. All of the dialects have in common the use of words to affirm one's spouse. Psychologist William James said that possibly the deepest human need is the need to feel appreciated. Words of affirmation will meet that need in many individuals.

Quality time

By "quality time," I mean giving someone your undivided attention. I don't mean sitting on the couch watching television together. When you spend time that way, Netflix or HBO has your attention — not your spouse. What I mean is sitting on the couch with the TV off, looking at each other and talking, devices put away, giving each other your undivided attention. Quality time means that you're attuned to each others' feelings, words, and body language and are responding in kind. It can also mean doing an activity together, such as taking a walk or going out to eat while having a heart-to-heart conversation.

Time is a precious commodity because the hours we all have in a day are limited. We all have multiple demands on our time, yet each of us has the exact same hours in a day. We can make the most of those hours by committing some of them to our partners/spouses. If your mate's primary love language is quality time, she simply wants you to be spending time with her.

Receiving gifts

Almost everything ever written on the subject of love indicates that at the heart of love is the spirit of giving. All five love languages challenge us to give to our spouse, but for some, receiving gifts speaks the loudest. Gifts are a visible symbol of love, and it might be why they carry more weight when expressing love.

A gift is something you can hold in your hand and say, "Look, he was thinking of me," or, "She remembered me." You must be thinking of someone to choose, buy, and then give them a gift. The gift itself is a symbol of that thought. It doesn't matter whether it costs money. What is important is that you thought of him or her. And it is not the thought implanted only in the mind that counts, but the thought expressed in actually securing the gift and giving it as the expression of love.

But what of the person who says, "I'm not the best gift-giver. I didn't receive many gifts growing up. I never learned how to select gifts. It doesn't come naturally for me." Well, now you know that you and your spouse speak different love languages. So, congratulations, you have just made the first discovery in becoming a great lover. Now that you have made that discovery, you can get on with the business of learning more love languages of yourself and your spouses. If your spouse's primary love language is receiving gifts, you can try to become at least a fair gift-giver. In fact, it is one of the easiest love languages to learn.

Acts of service

Michelle's primary love language was what I call "acts of service." By acts of service, I mean doing things you know your spouse would like you to do. You seek to please her by serving her, to express your love for her by doing things for her.

Consider simple activities such as cooking a meal, setting a table, emptying the dishwasher, vacuuming, changing the baby's diaper, picking up a prescription, and keeping the car in operating condition — they are all acts of service. They require thought, planning, time, effort, and energy. If done with a positive spirit, they are indeed expressions of love.

Besides figuring out the specific love languages of your spouse, you also need to examine and change stereotypes to express love more effectively. Remember, there are no rewards for maintaining stereotypes. However, there are tremendous benefits to meeting the emotional needs of your spouse. If your spouse's love language is acts of <u>service</u>, then "actions speak louder than words."

Physical touch

We have long known that physical touch is a way of communicating emotional love. Numerous research projects in the area of child development have made that conclusion: Babies who are held, stroked, and kissed develop a healthier emotional life than those who are left for long periods of time without physical contact. In fact, research has established that babies who are neglected (such as touch-starvation) are worse off than the ones who suffered active abuse.

Physical touch is also a powerful vehicle for communicating love between partners. Holding hands, embracing, and sexual intimacy are all ways of communicating emotional love to one's spouse. For some individuals, <u>physical touch</u> is their primary love language. Without it, they feel unloved. With it, their emotional tank is filled, and they feel secure in the love of their spouse.

Implicit love touches require little time but there are several considerations involved. Some people don't grow up in a lovey-touchy family, and as a result, they struggle with building physical intimacy with other adults. Also, if physical touch is not your primary love language or if you're touch-repulsed, it's going to be especially difficult to give that to others. However, you can work around these things. Physical touch can also look like sitting close to each other as you watch your favorite television program. Actions like these require no additional time and can communicate your love loudly. Touching your spouse as you walk through the room where he is sitting takes only a moment. Touching each other when you leave the house and again when you return may involve only a brief kiss or hug but will speak volumes to your spouse.

Once you discover that physical touch is the primary love language of your spouse, you are limited only by your imagination on ways to express love.

(https://www.focusonthefamily.com/marriage/communication-and-conflict/learn-to-speak-your-spouses-love-language/understanding-the-five-love-languages

The website below can be used to take the 5 Love Language Quiz to discover your love language. It has one for singles, childrenand couples.

(https://www.5lovelanguages.com/profile/)

As was said earlier, everything about Love is giving. When the focus in primarily on receiving, no longer is it love. For God so loved the world that he GAVE. It is not just giving. It means giving what the person needs and will match their language, and it means giving your best. If you have two pairs of shoes, one new and the other old, your best would be to give the new. Love is a gift that is freely given. Unconditional love doesn't make you feel like you need to earn it. It is never 'deserved' but always 'granted' freely. The person doesn't have to do anything to 'deserve' your love; their presence is enough.

The gift of love is given with ***focus, intensity, and energy***. These three things will guarantee that the person you are loving is convinced that you cherish, value, and care about them. Because love is a verb, it requires this targeted action. Love is also done and performed in a moment. Love is given in the moment in time. You cannot love someone yesterday, and you cannot love someone tomorrow. The only time you can love someone is in the moment. The problem at the moment that many people have are the thoughts that they are not lovable, worthless, can't get it right, undeserving and my fault, to name a few. Love needs to dominate during the toughest times in our lives. If you believe that you are not loved, you are mistaken. Seek love, and you will find it. Find someone to love, and see how it is returned to you.

Love, for some, can be scary. So many folks believe they have to 'do' things to 'earn' someone's love. This belief can show up in the way that you dress, the cologne you wear, how you spend money, and how you try to 'impress' others with things that, in a natural sense, aren't really you. Love is never deserved. If love is deserved, it means that it is 'worked for'; this is not love, but it is called a 'wage. You work for a wage, but love is always freely given. It is given, with nothing expected in return. Many young couples are struggling with love because of their expectations of getting something in return. These expectations often determine the amount and quality of the love they give. If you know that you are getting something, you're prone to give more love. If there is doubt, it seems to be held back. Look at what Luke 6:32-34 says about this:

For if ye love them which love you, what thank have ye? for sinners also love those that love them.

33 And if ye do good to them which do good to you, what thank have ye? for sinners also do even the same.

34 And if ye lend to them of whom ye hope to receive, what thank have ye? for sinners also lend to sinners, to receive as much again.

The other thing about love is that it is impossible to love someone unless you allow yourself to be **vulnerable**. Otherwise, it's like trying to hug a cactus! Very difficult to get close to. True love makes room for closeness and is a safe space that lets people show up as they are. Love tells the truth in a way that causes growth and encouragement. It exudes kindness, but not in a way so you can be used as a doormat where people can trample over you and your love.

Trauma and 'junk' that causes emotional dysregulation can make us believe that we have no hope in life. God is more than willing and able to love you no matter what condition you may believe that you are in.

More often than not, loving someone or allowing someone to love you is a challenge. This difficulty often arises because of the history of hurt and the future worry of being hurt again. The next chapter describes a relational 'skeleton' of what causes the most conflicts, especially in a couple's relationship.

<u>Reflection Prompts</u>

- What is your primary love language? How do you express and receive love?

- Reflect on a moment when love felt challenging. How did you overcome that challenge?

- Write about the difference between "feeling love" and "choosing to love."

CHAPTER: 7

MARRIAGE AND CONFLICTS

We live in a world where divorces are increasing at an alarmingly high rate and the reasons could be traced back to the reasons that people initially get married for. Out of the various reasons, one might be that the person is physically attractive or that the other person is a good listener. It could also be for reasons like using that person as a rebound from a previously bad relationship or to have sex. Some people even get married just because they are bored and have the 'get while the getting is good' mindset. It could also be just out of desperation and loneliness. One's external appearance might be what attracts us to each other, but it's what is on the inside, like character, strengths, and positive core beliefs, that will keep us together.

When done right, marriage is a phenomenal thing. It's two people coming together as one to exercise their ability to demonstrate love at the highest level. There is nothing like being loved in a way that convinces you how important you are to each other. Love is a great thing to experience; there's almost nothing that compares to it! I see a lot of couples who are struggling with this concept of loving each other in an effective, convincing manner. I have developed a theory that may be helpful regarding what causes relationships to wane and lose their energy. This process is targeted at what causes these conflicts and what causes couples to become polarized. We will be going over the concept of polarization later.

Expectations

↓

Resentment

↓

Fear

EXPECTATIONS

Because we all grow up differently, we have different expectations of love and being loved. The values we currently practice are mostly derived from all the people who have been a part of our lives. These people can range from our parents, aunts, uncles, grandparents, pastors, gang members, and teachers, to name a few. These experiences with these relationships teach us our values and mold our character; this can also be referred to as conditioning. We learn how to move about in our society. Albert Bandura, creator of Social Learning Theory, says it like this: *Behavior is learned from the environment through the process of observational learning.*

(https://www.simplypsychology.org/bandura.htm)

We're all a product of how we grew up. We cannot help how we, as children, grew up. We just grew up as life intended and learned whatever we could and however we could. Our upbringing shaped how we view life, trust, relationships, society, the world, and our community. No two people grow up the same way, even if they grew up in the same town or the same neighborhood. Because of how we grew up, we have developed different needs. These needs are tailored by the influential people in our formative years. We have learned to do things in a certain way because it 'makes sense' to do them that way based on what we learned and what we were taught.

This point is especially important with it comes to relationships. Sometimes, people believe that two people should be the same. I believe that it is the differences that bring vibrancy, color, and excitement to a relationship, not just the similarities. Ask yourself, would you marry yourself? Most of you would probably decline the proposal from yourself. However, if you are narcissistic, you may exhibit so-and-so behaviors. We do things that feel safe or familiar based on how we grew up. For example, in a couple's relationship, it makes sense to wash the cup when you're done with it. It makes sense to bring your underwear out of the bathroom after taking a shower. It makes sense to put gas in your vehicle **before** you bring it home. It makes sense to squeeze the toothpaste from the end and not the middle. It makes sense to do it that way. But with relationships, the problem with expectations is that about 80% of expectations are unspoken (guess-ta-mation). These expectations cause problems because we start applying them to everyone, and then "it makes sense" for everyone to do things that way.

Expectations are like needs. People may say that they go into a relationship not expecting anything, but I beg to differ. We marry and have a relationship with certain people because of how they fill our needs. We are emotionally and relationally fed by that person in a way that no one else does. That's why we choose what we choose because we like what we like.

When two people first meet each other, the goal is to fill each other's needs to the max. They go out of their way to fill the needs of this potential mate; they open car doors and take them to fancy restaurants. Laughing at their ridiculous jokes, letting them 'get away' with snide remarks, etc. They continue to feed each other like a peanut butter and jelly sandwich with too much jelly, the jelly dripping from the sides! There is nothing like being loved genuinely. There is a song that indicates that often, people look for love in all the wrong places. But the fact remains that they are looking for love. Teddy Pendergrass said that:

It's so good, good lovin' somebody
And that somebody loves you back, and that's a fact
It's so good wantin' somebody
And that somebody wants you back

(https://www.bing.com/search?q=feels+so+good+loving+somebo
dy+loves+you+back+lyrics&qs=NW&pq=feels+so+good+loving+
somebody+loves+you+back+ly&sc=1-
47&cvid=D8C6FF3E05BD4040AB1AE8985D928307&FORM=Q
BRE&sp=1)

On the positive side, if a couple or family can communicate their expectations/needs effectively, it can spark a genuine connection. Connection flourishes from honest communication, not from a dictatorial set of demands.

The good, the bad, and the ugly in a marriage or connection is what makes them work well in reality. Often people want to stay like it 'was when we first met', believing that all will be ok. Yet, nothing when it's stagnant and unchanging. Marriages, just like people, grow. In that growth it takes attention, intention, and mindfulness about said growth. Inevitably, people will go through changes and it is to those changes of maturity that partners need to accommodate each other. Change doesn't always have to signify leaving something because it doesn't meet your expectations/needs like it used to. Some people believe that this means that after owning a car for some years, you have to trade it in for a new model. Even worse, some people apply this concept to friends and partners, too. But that is the farthest thing that needs to happen! Change and adjustments to it are essential to a marriage, just like to people. The ingredient that makes a marriage meaningful is how it has evolved.

When two people first meet, everything is rosy and full of energy. For some, this is known as the 'Honeymoon" phase. But, as with all good things, change has to occur. There is a business model of change that we need to look at. The first part of change is **Discomfort**. It would be safe to say that no one likes discomfort. This discomfort is comprised of a lot of feelings like anger, anxiety, depression, insecurity, sadness, etc. This discomfort comes from life events, life's 'stuff', or just living. Things do not remain the same. The degree of discomfort depends on the degree of change. It is virtually impossible for there to be change without discomfort. There is an old gym saying, "No Pain, No Gain". There is some truth to that in terms of relationships as well. I am not suggesting that you go out there and actively seek out discomfort just so you can grow.

On the contrary, the discomfort will more than likely find you! The next part of change is **Growth**. The change and discomfort eventually alchemize into growth. This growth occurs because of the change. Flowering plants **do not** thrive if the weather is 78 degrees and sunny every day; this would not encourage growth. It is the winds, the rain, and the cold temperatures that cause the plants to grow. The differing weather causes the roots to grow deeper, the bark to become stronger, and the old leaves to fall off in order to produce new ones. Scott Peck, author and psychiatrist, describes love as: he will to extend one's self for the purpose of nurturing one's own or another's spiritual growth.

Similarly, marriages go through seasonal growth and change. Mature couples realize the changes and the discomfort and are willing to change accordingly for the sake of their loved ones. They realize that the relationship is changing for the better as it matures. The last part of this process is **Opportunity**. When changes occur through discomfort and growth is allowed to happen, opportunities for flourishment in the relationship are present. Opportunities to see each other better, to love better, to grow better together, to receive blessings, and to rid themselves of things that are causing stagnation and polarization. Too often, people resist change, which causes stagnation. Change is a decision made.

Change allows us to be their 'best' for their mate. When you first met, you presented yourself as your best. You wore your best clothes, had good manners and good attentiveness skills, and did your best to have your mate gravitate closer to you. Why does that have to change? There's always room for improvement in terms of presentation, manners, attentiveness skills, and desiring our mates to gravitate closer to us! There's growth in changes for the better. We certainly don't want our children to stay at the age of 4! We want them to grow and mature and to become productive. As they grow, we need to adjust how we treat them and adjust to the change in the relationship. We can't treat our 14-year-olds as if they were 5. So, as children do, marriage grows in years of maturity as well. You don't want to treat each other like you did two years into the marriage when you have been together for 8 years. You want it to mature and be BETTER!

Unfortunately, a relationship won't always go the way you want it to. Things happen, connection is disrupted, and distance occurs. Arguments ensue, and conflict can seem to dominate. Every couple will have arguments and conflicts. But mature relationships do not allow these things to linger. They find a way to communicate through their struggles and find a way to resolve things. Mature couples will let love and connection dominate. The immature relationships will often avoid accountability and play the blame game that stops them from growing. For instance, they might use sentences like, "If you would just do that thing that I asked, everything would be all right!" Folks can throw such lines around when they blame others for the discord. There is an old saying that goes like this: It takes two people to cause connection and only one person to cause discord.

Just like people have a role in getting together, they have a role in breaking apart. I have observed while working with couples that some things are considered absolute 'deal-breakers'. These are things that will get in the way of doing meaningful couple's work even if couples wish to reconcile. These are things like infidelity (especially ongoing), domestic violence, ongoing drug addiction, chronic/debilitating mental illness, and when the two parties aren't in agreement on reestablishing and connected relationship. Other than these, the two people have a role in the conflict. When we talk about conflict, these are not the 'petty' life items. We don't mean forgetting to put gas in the car, talking down to the mother-in-law, or ordering the wrong pizza. The conflict is in the relationship itself and not anything outside of it. When a couple fights/argues, it's NEVER about what it's about, but it's always about what it MEANS. It is this core part of the relationship that needs adjusting. People will always have contradictory views about things. People will always have differences in a relationship. So, an argument about the differences can be anticipated. It is the unmet needs that keep a relationship secure that is the core of a maturing relationship. There is a role that both parties play in this relational distance or polarization. It is hard to be close when there is distance.

It's like trying to drink water while keeping your mouth closed; it's quite a difficult task. The destructive part of not owning up to your role in the discord is what causes injury.

Then there are folks in relationships called 'Right Fighters". These are folks who have to be right about everything and wish to have the 'last word' whenever there is a conflict. They are normally arrogant, unbearable, and unteachable. However, there is a consolation prize with the Right Fighter in that they are sometimes right. Because they have to be right all the time, they often forget about the consequences of the process of being right all the time. Their stubborn attitude and will to be right all the time often leave a lot of casualties behind. You can see the damage just by looking at the faces of the children and their mates when they are fighting to be right! These people will not take responsibility for their role in the relational distance.

As both people have a role in discord, there is a role in the reunification. There is a saying that was given to me years ago, and I would like to share: **The value of a person to you determines the intensity of the fight you put in for that person**. The value of your mate determines how much you will fight to keep a close bond with them. The value of your mate to you has to override differences, petty arguments, and the occasional distancing. The value of that person will allow love to overcome everything else. The marriage must not let pride or anger become their decision-maker. God never created our emotions to be our decision-makers. It is the executive portion of our body, our brains, that should be the determinant in our decision-making. Just like our values, our self-esteem is based on what we know and believe about ourselves, so should we make decisions about the relationship? There is a role and responsibility We have to cause the relationship to flourish.

Often, we tell each other what we 'think' about each other rather than what we 'believe' about each other. In the conversation, we may tell our mate what we think about their driving, food choices, the content they watch, their wardrobe, or their favorite football team. Couples who flourish will more often talk about what they believe about each other. These beliefs are what bring and keep the relationship together. These are not often talked about with intent. Beliefs are things like being loving, safe, handsome, beautiful, sexy, peaceful, likable, respectful, satisfying, hard-worker, funny, fun, 'mine', honest, dependable, etc. Think of what would happen to couples if their conversations were dominated by these beliefs that they have about each other! Too often, the conversations and attitudes are dominated by what they think about each other. These 'thoughts' are often accompanied by certain colorful metaphors, to say it gently!

The ultimate goal of the relationship is connectedness. Our society has often defined a committed relationship as two people learning how to *coexist*. However, I disagree. I think that this isn't a definition of a committed relationship. *The definition of a committed relationship has to be two people learning how to connect.* It is in this connection that you will find love, peace, happiness, safety, respect, and closeness.

Reflection Prompts

- How do you balance worldly challenges with spiritual growth?

- Reflect on your favorite Bible verse or hymn. How does it inspire your journey?

- Write a prayer or letter to God about an area in your life where you seek growth or clarity.

Assertive Communication

PSYCHOLOGY TOOLS

Assertive communication means clearly and calmly expressing what you want

without either being too passive or too aggressive. Learning to communicate

assertively doesn't guarantee you will have your needs met, but it makes it more likely, and it can improve your relationships with other people.

http://psychology.tools

Passive	Assertive	Aggressive
Give in	Compromise	Take
Not talking, not being heard	Talking and listening	Talking over people
Trying to keep the peace	Making sure things are fair - for you and others	Looking out for yourself
Allowing yourself to be bullied	Standing up for yourself	Bullying others
Not saying what you think, or not saying anything	Express your point clearlyand confidently	Can lead to shouting, aggression, or violence
Damages relationships – other people respect you less	Enhances relationships – other people know where they stand	Damages relationships – other people don't like aggression
Damages your self-esteem	Builds your self-esteem	Damages others self-esteem

Tips for communicating assertively

- Use "I" statements

- Be clear and direct:

"I would like you to give me a refund."

"I think what you have done is good, but I would like to see more of..."

- Describe how another person's *behavior* makes you *feel* so other people are aware of the consequences of their actions:

"When you raise your voice, it makes me scared ... I would like you to speak softly."

"When you don't tell me what you are feeling, it makes me confused."

- Stick to your guns - the broken record technique. This technique involves thinking about what you want, preparing what you might say,

and then repeating it as necessary:

"I would like a refund ... Yes, but I would still like a refund ... I've heard what you have said, but I still want a refund."

COMMUNICATION

It is important to 'slow down' the intensity of the possible conflict in terms of thinking and language.

1. Wait a minute and take a breath.

2. I noticed _____ (a behavior)

3. What just happened?

What changed?

What's Different?

4. What do you need that will help you in this moment?

The goal is for the conversation to stop or to slow down about the 'item/issue' and the focus to be redirected to tending to each other's needs. My mother would often tell me never to make a permanent decision based on a temporary situation because all situations are temporary.

<u>RESENTMENT</u>

Another thing in the relational process that causes conflict is resentment. Resentment is defined as *the feeling of displeasure or indignation at some act, remark, person, etc., regarded as causing injury or insult.*

<u>https://www.dictionary.com/browse/resentment</u>}

At the beginning of a relationship, I compare it to 'fun food'. It makes you smile, and it satisfies your desires, but it is typically not healthy for you, nor does it have much in the way of nutritional value. Many relationships start in this way: fun food. But over a while, the relationship has to grow, and the fun food is no longer nutritional enough for relational growth.

So, over a period of time, those expectations start to lose focus. Something tends to interrupt the 'bliss' of the fun food aspect of the relationship. Relationally, resentment says: "At one time, you met my needs. You met my needs with focus, intent, and energy. I didn't have to ask, beg, or even give it a second thought that you would be there to meet my needs. Because I know that you have the capability to meet my needs like no other, and my needs aren't being met now, I believe it is on purpose that you are neglecting to meet my needs. I often believe that you have the intent to hurt me, to harm me, or to maim me. I believe and feel this because, at one point in time, you met my needs willingly, but now it is a willful action to withhold meeting my needs."

So, how do you know when resentment is there? You hear conversations starting with the phrase, 'You used to'. You used to hold my hands. You used to bring me flowers. You used to cook my favorite meal. You used to tell me I look good. You used to sit next to me. You used to be proud of me. This voice comes from the part of us that is starving to be loved and for their needs to be met. This voice comes from the part of us that's uncertain when their needs will be met by their mate. This voice is of a desperate and hungry part of you that doesn't know if it will ever be satiated again. There is nothing cooking in the emotional kitchen. Another phrase you will hear is 'if'. If you love me, if you cared about me, if I meant something to you, if I was important to you; This, too, is the voice of someone who is starving and needs desperately to be filled by the one they chose, out of all of the people in the world, to feed them. It's like going to your favorite restaurant only to find that they have 'chosen' to stop cooking. That's just bad business!

FEAR

Resentment, as devastating as it is in a relationship, it's not the worst thing that can happen in this relational process that causes conflict. When resentment has done its 'dirty work,' fear is born. Fear is defined as a distressing emotion aroused by impending danger, evil, pain, etc., whether the threat is real or imagined; the feeling or condition of being afraid.

(https://www.dictionary.com/browse/fear?s=t)

Relationally, I need to take this a step further. In this sense, fear is not an emotion but a belief system. Instead of representing love, joy, peace, contentment, and safety, now their mate represents hurt and pain. Fear is the belief that hurt and pain is near. Fear tells you that it is time to find cover or fight. Fear is also a toxic word. In essence, fear degrades, deteriorates, and destroys essential parts of the relationship. How do we know that fear is in the relationship? You want to isolate, or you have this need to fight. The only reason you would want to do these actions is because there is a believable threat. The person will measure their words because they cannot say what's on their heart for fear of reprisals. They take the long way home so that they spend little time. They start to do solitary things in their life. The figure below tells us what fear looks like in a relationship that is filled with conflict.

On a side note, scared, afraid, and frightened are emotions at come from fear. On a side note, the four scariest things in the world are:

1. Something

2. Anything

3. Everything

4. The Unknown

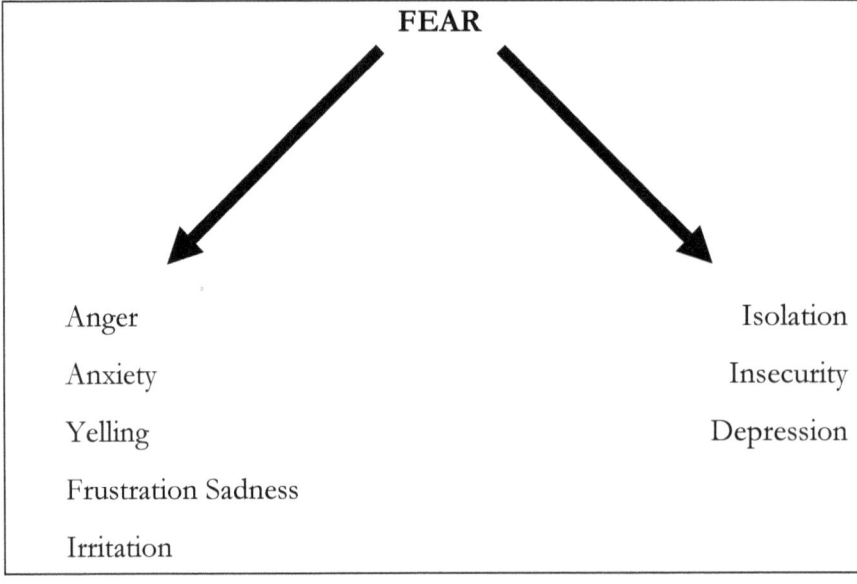

The anger, anxiety, yelling, frustration, and irritation side of the matrix is an attempt to eliminate the fear, hurt, and pain. When someone wrongs us, we tend to get angry. When we see a dog coming at us, we tend to yell. When someone becomes a threat in our life, we tend to be frustrated and maybe even anxious when they are in our presence. The yelling is an attempt to get the person who represents hurt and pain to back off. Typically, when a couple 'look for a fight', it is an attempt to control that person who represents fear in their lives. The isolation and depression part of the matrix is an attempt to 'hide' from the hurt and pain. They will be quiet, avoid the person, work long hours, focus on the children and avoid contact.

Remember that fear is a toxic word that degrades and destroys the two essential parts of the relationship. The parts of the relationship that fear affects the most are ***Love and Trust***. You don't get to see a demonstration of Love, nor do you get to experience Trust. Second Timothy 1:7 tells us: For God has not given us a **spirit** of **fear, but** of power and of love and of a **sound mind**.

The antidote for the fear in the marriage is to create emotional safety in the relationship. Marriage is an emotional system. Much like the respiratory and circulatory systems in our body, marriage is an emotional system. Even though love is not a feeling, feelings occur because of the decision to love someone. There is a bible verse in Matthew that Jesus tells us that man cannot live by bread alone but by every word that proceeds out of the mouth of God.

Similarly, I don't believe that we can live by emotions alone, either. When we are influenced too much by our emotions, it leads to chaos in our lives. Depending on your emotions will not stabilize you. You will become unstable, like a Dixie cup in the wind!

Even so, emotions are a part of life, and they are great to experience. We often experience these emotions more so with our close family, friends, and marital partners. Many people have had negative experiences in their lives. These negative experiences could be betrayal, divorce, trauma, abuse, losses, and abandonment, to name a few. Along with these experiences comes an associated emotion. We often don't notice the emotions, but our body and mind does. We may experience anger at these experiences, but anger is also another word for HURT. When we are angry, it is often because we have been hurt. We experience continued anger when we believe we have been mistreated as well.

CHAPTER: 8

CREATING EMOTIONAL SAFETY

This is an excerpt from Focus On The Family

https://www.focusonthefamily.com/marriage/creating-a-safe-marriage/

Create

The best approach to foster intimacy and deep connection after an argument is to focus time, attention and energy on creating relational space that feels safe. When your spouse feels safe, he is naturally inclined to relax and open his heart. In this peaceful state, connection simply happens. You don't have to force intimacy or connection when you feel safe. I believe this to be true because God designed our hearts to be open. The default setting of a heart is openness. This belief is also very prevalent in the Eastern spiritual belief systems, such as the Awakened Heart in Buddhism. It takes much more effort and energy to keep our hearts shut down than to let them stay open.

Think about a recent time when your spouse hurt or frustrated you. Remember how quickly your heart shut down? Once your heart closed, you instantly reacted in some way (fight-or-flight) and ultimately disconnected altogether. But remember, your heart was not designed to stay closed. Maintaining a closed heart is like trying to force a huge beach ball underwater. You have to strain and push to keep a ball full of air underwater. It's the same with your heart. You have to work really hard to keep a heart full of God's love shut down. Have you ever noticed, when your spouse takes responsibility for her actions and seeks forgiveness, how quickly your heart opens back up? Like that beach ball under the water, once you feel safe, your heart will burst back open. You can go from feeling shut down to instantly feeling connected and open.

Emotional safety sets a peaceful environment that allows people to relax. Hence, in your quest for reconnection after an argument, I want to encourage you to make creating safety a top priority. Hopefully, you now see that the only way to become one is to intertwine two open hearts together.

Creating Safety for Open Hearts

A heart will open only when it feels safe. But what does feeling safe really mean? Listen to some of these answers:

- Feeling completely secure
- Being accepted for who I am
- Feeling relaxed and comfortable
- Being free to express who I really am
- Being loved unconditionally
- Feeling respected
- Knowing that my spouse is trustworthy
- Having my spouse be there for me
- Being fully understood
- Being valued and honored
- Having loving reassurance
- Being able to fully open yourself in order to give and receive love
- Not being judged
- Being seen for who I am
- Having my flaws accepted as part of the whole package
- Living in an atmosphere of open communication

Wouldn't it be amazing for these things to be the foundation of marriage? Feeling emotionally safe is critical for a marriage to thrive.

I define emotional safety as feeling free to open up and reveal who you really are while trusting that the other person will still love, value, and unconditionally accept you. In other words, you feel safe with someone when you are confident and trust that he or she will handle your heart – your deepest feelings, thoughts, desires, hopes, and dreams – with the utmost care. So, how do we build a marriage that feels like the safest place on earth?

Emotional safety is not simply a bunch of psychobabble. Safety is, first and foremost, something that our heavenly Father provides for us.

- The name of the LORD is a strong tower; the righteous run to it and are safe. (Proverbs 18:10)

- Keep me safe, O God, for in you I take refuge. (Psalm 16:1)

- In peace, I will lie down and sleep, for you alone, LORD, make me dwell in safety. (Psalm 4:8)

These are just a few of the many verses that show how the God of this universe goes out of His way to make us feel safe. He wants our hearts open so He can love through us. And hearts open when they feel safe. The safest relationship we will ever have is with our heavenly Father. I want to model my earthly relationships after what God does with me. The key to creating a marriage that feels like the safest place on earth is found in Ephesians 5:29: "For no one ever hated his own flesh, but nourishes and cherishes it, just as Christ also does the church." Creating a safe marriage involves both an attitude and an action. *Cherishing* is the right attitude, and *nourishing* is the powerful action.

Cherish

The primary attitude that will help your spouse feel emotionally safe is when he believes that you understand how incredibly valuable he is. That is the essence of honor. Honor is a decision to view our spouse as a priceless treasure – one of high worth and value. King Solomon encouraged this as well: "A man's greatest treasure is his wife." (Proverbs 18:22).

Honor isn't based on behavior or subject to emotion. You grant your spouse value whether they want it or deserve it. Honor is a decision you make and a gift you give. Apostle Paul encouraged the early Christians to practice this when he wrote, "Be devoted to one another in brotherly love; give preference to one another in honor" (Romans 12:10).

God has made it resplendently clear that our wife/husband is valuable. Look at some of the verses that show how much our heavenly Father values and cherishes us:

- "For you Were made in my image." (Genesis 1:27)
- "I chose you when I planned creation." (Ephesians 1:11)
- "You are fearfully and wonderfully made." (Psalm 139:14)
- "For you are my treasured possession." (Exodus 19:5)

It's amazing to think that the God of this universe considers our spouse His treasured possession. That's powerful! However, when couples are in the midst of an argument, and the heart closes, the first thing to go is the awareness of his/her incredible value.

And in those moments, when we fail to see them as our heavenly Father sees His daughter/son, we're not safe. When we lose sight of their value, when we're not cherishing him/her, we are more apt to react and treat them in dishonoring ways. Then our mate has every right to put up a wall and protect them self.

It's also what my father does to get his heart back open. Luke 12:34 explains why it is so powerful: "For where your treasure is, so there will your heart be also." In other words, your heart will be open to what you value. One way to keep your heart open and your spouse feeling safe with you is to focus on her values.

We can create this honor list for our spouse as well. Take several minutes to list all the reasons why your spouse is so valuable. For example, a character trait, faith pattern, values, morals, parenting skills, spirituality, the roles he or she plays that you appreciate (worker, friend, parent, sibling, son), personality characteristics, how he or she treats you, etc.

And don't keep the amazing list to yourself – share it with your spouse. Let her know that you recognize her value. When this happens, not only does your spouse benefit, but you are positively impacted as well.

Nourish

Understanding your spouse's incredible value is the beginning of safety. However, to create a marriage that feels like the safest place on earth, you must be able to express honor through action and behavior. "Let us not love with mere words or tongue but with actions and in truth" (1 John 3:18). Honor in action means that you learn how to handle your spouse's heart — her deepest feelings, thoughts, and desires — with the utmost care. You need to visualize his heart tattooed with the words "Handle with care."

Remember, "emotional safety" is feeling free to open up and reveal who you really are and trust that the other person will still love, value, and accept you. As you can see, the last part of the definition communicates a powerful message: "You are incredibly valuable, so don't be afraid of letting me see your heart. You can share your deepest feelings, thoughts, opinions, hopes, dreams, fears, hurts, and memories, and I will still love and accept you."

Let me make practical the idea of safety in action. Jackson and Krista, a married couple attending a marriage training seminar, were just about to discuss a big fight they were having around the remodeling of their home. At this moment, Jackson didn't care what Krista knew or what was going on with her. His heart was closed; he didn't feel safe. But instead of trying to get Jackson to care about her pain and frustration, Krista made it her goal to care about Jackson's heart. "I so greatly appreciate your sense of responsibility and the fact that when you say you're going to do something, it will always happen," Krista started. "You are such a man of integrity. I think this is why I've been confused about the lack of follow-through around this remodel. Would you be willing to help me understand what is going on for you?"

When you **choose** to care for your spouse, it can instantly create a safe environment to share your deepest thoughts and feelings.

"You're right," Jackson cautiously responded. "I'm usually great at follow-through. But this project has made me realize just how inadequate I am around home repair. My dad is so great at it. As a builder, John (a family friend) is amazing. I think I realized that I couldn't do anything without their help. That made me feel like a failure. Since this is our first house, I want to feel competent. I want you to trust that if something breaks, I can fix it without having to call my dad or some repairman."

Krista instantly held Jackson's hand tight in her own and, with tears in her eyes, smiled at her husband. "That makes so much sense," she said gently. "I had no idea that you felt this way. I am so sorry that you have been feeling like a failure."

This is the power of safety in action. Caring has the power to soften a closed heart. The key to putting caring into action is compassion. And Krista was willing to do that for Jackson. King Solomon said it best: "Words from a wise man's mouth are gracious" (Ecclesiastes 10:12). Another word for "gracious" as it's used here is "compassionate." The verse could also read, "Words from a wise man's mouth are compassionate."

Certainly, compassion is an important first step to moving from unhealthy conflict into intimacy. Just ask Jackson. Allow your spouse's pain that was caused by your argument to drive you to a place of compassion. Make your first goal to alleviate their hurt and emotional pain. When We come together to talk about conflict, we can use compassion to help our spouse feel cared for. Doing this creates instant safety. A heart will open when it feels safe.

Your compassion communicates that your spouse's heart matters to you. How do you express that you value your spouse's heart? The best way to communicate compassion is to follow Krista's lead — through a kind look, a gentle word, a soft touch, or caring actions. Care and compassion break down the opposition and create two open hearts. And when you create the right atmosphere through emotional safety, you have unlocked the door of healthy conflict.

https://www.focusonthefamily.com/marriage/creating-a-safe-marriage/

Believe

To emphasize it once again, we don't live a life based on what we think but rather on what we *believe*. Our beliefs determine our focus in life and the direction we go in life. When we have negative core beliefs, it causes our direction to become unstable and misplaced. Sadly, we didn't form these beliefs knowingly. These beliefs might have once served us in the past in some way or helped us survive. Most of these negative core beliefs result from negative life experiences such as bullying, traumatic events, losses, betrayals, and abandonments, to name a few.

Some examples of negative beliefs are: My Fault, Not Safe, Guilty, Can't Get It Right, Unlovable, Worthless, Baggage Carrier, Can't Trust, Performance-Based, and Gotta Get It Right. These beliefs or labels can carry folks in a debilitating place I call the infamous 'Rabbit Hole'. The Rabbit Hole is a dark place and nothing good is found in that rabbit hole. It is dirty, muddy, full of feces, and extremely dark. The Rabbit Hole can also be considered our shadow, where the discarded or scowled parts of ourselves dwell. Though it's not a place of comfort or positivity, it's worth taking a stroll around once in a while to check what atrocities are lurking there that we need to get rid of. (basically what work we need to do on ourselves)

The interesting thing about these negative core beliefs is that none of them are true. They cannot be proven as being the truth about you. Now, many will say that each person has their individual truth. I disagree with this notion. The definition of truth is A Restatement of Facts or Faith (you shall know the truth, and the truth shall make you free). Ask yourself, can you prove any of the above beliefs with facts, or are you using your emotions and/or opinions to justify these beliefs?

Point: An assumption and an opinion need two things to stand: 1. A crowd and 2. A lot of emotions. The truth needs one thing to stand: It needs to be said/spoken.

CHAPTER: 9

BOUNDARIES

Boundaries are a wonderful thing, especially for fostering relationships. Boundaries teach others how to treat us. If we are being treated a certain way by others, chances are, we taught them and allowed them how to treat us that way. And I don't mean 'formal' teaching moments. Letting people do certain things or letting them get away with something in our presence that we don't like or agree with are signs of weak personal boundaries. Some examples are:

1. *Saying no when you mean yes and yes when you mean no,*

2. *feeling guilty when you say no,*

3. *allowing others to touch you inappropriately without any objection,*

4. *allowing others to say things in front of you that make you uncomfortable,*

5. *not communicating your emotional needs in your closest relationships,*

6. *becoming overly involved with the issues of others so that you are accepted or perceived as being useful or important,*

7. *not speaking up with you have something to say.*

An essential component of healthy relationships is creating and maintaining boundaries. Boundaries get misunderstood because the name indicates that we might want to restrict our relationships. However, most times, when we put boundaries in place, it's an attempt to keep certain people in our lives, just in a way that honors us too. People who don't 'stand' and exercise their boundaries usually attract needy, greedy, disrespectful, and controlling people in their lives. When people 'give in' to someone negotiating their boundaries, they actually train others to treat them in a certain manner or just to take advantage of them. Each time we do not stand, it chips away at our self-respect and the respect that others may have for us. When we do not exercise boundaries, we are left in a state of insecurity. People may start to question themselves and may look to other sources to validate their importance and self-worth.

There are three main elements to Boundaries:

1. A boundary isn't a boundary unless it is *Identified.*

2. A boundary isn't a boundary unless it is *Communicated.*

3. A boundary isn't a boundary unless it is *Enforced.*

This is called **ICE**. The primary force that identifies, communicates, and enforces are boundaries is our *self-worth.* People with low self-worth tend to have boundaries like 'Swiss cheese'. These boundaries are porous, meaning they have a lot of holes. There's nothing guarding them to determine what comes in or what gets taken out. People with low self-worth tend to allow energy-stealing items to infiltrate their hearts and minds, which tends to influence their decision-making. Typically, what ends up happening is that they start basing their decisions on their need to be validated by others and the external world.

Our self-worth must not be defined as how we 'feel' about ourselves. Never! Our emotions are challenged every day, and the events that challenge them seem to be mostly out of our control and happen out of nowhere. They are not predictable. We could get an alarming text, a strange phone call, or meet someone at work with a bad attitude. We could get some bad news. Maybe the temperature in the office is colder than normal, or we might have had a bad chili dog for lunch. All of these unexpected events can steer our emotions in different directions. Whatever emotional state we are in, our self-worth should be the foundation of what we know and believe about ourselves, not our feelings.

This belief keeps us stable even through the challenging times in our lives. Our character and what we believe is our strength. If you believe you are an honest person, you will live aligned with this attribute of your personality, hence reinforcing it. If you have an opportunity to be dishonest, your 'conscious' will remind you that this is not us. By contrast, if we believe that we are 'worthless' or 'not good enough', we will reinforce this belief each day as well. **We do not live a life based on what we think. We live a life based on what we believe.** It is important to note that our beliefs are what fuel our strength and character. By contrast, the Fruit of the Spirit details the character of a Christian. The below internet article came from Bibleinfo.

(https://www.bibleinfo.com/en/questions/fruit-of-the-spirit)

The fruit of the Spirit, found in Galatians 5:22-23, is made up of the following nine qualities or gifts: love, joy, peace, patience, kindness, goodness, faithfulness, gentleness, and self-control.

Fruit of the Spirit list:

1. *Love*

2. *Joy*

3. *Peace*

4. *Patience*

5. *Kindness*

6. *Goodness*

7. *Faithfulness*

8. *Gentleness*

9. *Self-control*

Love

"Love is patient, love is kind. It does not envy, it does not boast, it is not proud. It does not dishonor others, it is not self-seeking, it is not easily angered, it keeps no record of wrongs. Love does not delight in evil but rejoices with the truth. It always protects, always trusts, always hopes, always perseveres" (1 Corinthians 13:4-7, NIV).

"And above all things have fervent love for one another, for 'love will cover a multitude of sins'" (1 Peter 4:8).

Joy

"Rejoice in the Lord always; again I will say, rejoice" (Philippians 4:4)!

"Rejoice always; pray without ceasing; in everything give thanks; for this is God's will for you in Christ Jesus" (1 Thessalonians 5:16-18).

"Now may the God of hope fill you with all joy and peace in believing, so that you will abound in hope by the power of the Holy Spirit" (Romans 15:13).

Peace

"You will keep him in perfect peace, whose mind is stayed on You, because he trusts in You" (Isaiah 26:3, NKJV).

"Be anxious for nothing, but in everything by prayer and supplication with thanksgiving, let your requests be made known to God. And the peace of God, which surpasses all comprehension, will guard your hearts and your minds in Christ Jesus" (Philippians 4:6-7).

"Let the peace of Christ rule in your hearts, to which indeed you Were called in one body; and be thankful" (Colossians 3:15).

Patience

"Rest in the LORD and wait patiently for Him; do not fret because of him who prospers in his way, because of the man who carries out wicked schemes" (Psalm 37:7).

"Here is the patience of the saints; here are those who keep the commandments of God and the faith of Jesus" (Revelation 14:12, NKJV).

"The Lord is not slow about His promise, as some count slowness, but is patient toward you, not wishing for any to perish but for all to come to repentance" (2 Peter 3:9).

Kindness

"Be kind to one another, tender-hearted, forgiving each other, just as God in Christ also has forgiven you" (Ephesians 4:32).

"Those who are kind benefit themselves, but the cruel bring ruin on themselves" (Proverbs 11:17, NIV).

"Love is patient, love is kind..." (1 Corinthians 13:4).

Goodness

"Surely goodness and lovingkindness will follow me all the days of my life, and I will dwell in the house of the LORD forever" (Psalm 23:6).

"Who among you is wise and understanding? Let him show by his good behavior his deeds in the gentleness of wisdom" (James 3:13).

"Do not remember the sins of my youth or my transgressions; according to Your lovingkindness, remember me, for Your goodness' sake, O LORD" (Psalm 25:7).

Faithfulness

"A faithful man will abound with blessings, but he who makes haste to be rich will not go unpunished" (Proverbs 28:20).

"For We walk by faith, not by sight" (2 Corinthians 5:7).

"Most men will proclaim each his own goodness, but who can find a faithful man" (Proverbs 20:6, NKJV)?

Gentleness

"Let your gentleness be evident to all. The Lord is near" (Philippians 4:5, NIV).

"...to be peaceable, gentle, showing every consideration for all men" (Titus 3:2).

"A gentle answer turns away wrath, but a harsh word stirs up anger" (Proverbs 15:1).

Self-control

"Like a city that is broken into and without walls is a man who has no control over his spirit" (Proverbs 25:28).

"He who is slow to anger is better than the mighty, and he who rules his spirit, than he who captures a city" (Proverbs 16:32).

"The end of all things is near; therefore, be of sound judgment and sober spirit for the purpose of prayer" (1 Peter 4:7).

Along with boundaries come emotions. These emotions are attached to our self-worth. We can 'feel' good about ourselves when we make decisions based on our self-worth or idea of self. On the other hand, we will feel bad or remorseful when we do things that are outside of our character. Emotions are not our enemy; we just need to realize what's the root of the emotion. Most times, our emotions are manageable, just as long as we realize that our emotions are reactions to the current happenings of our lives. Emotions are supposed to come and pass. When we allow our past or historical attitudes to muddle our emotional lives, it tends to intensify our emotional outbursts.

I need to talk to you, very briefly, about anger. I think two things cause us to get angry;

1. A violation of our values

2. An attack on our self-esteem.

When someone, or we ourselves, violate one of our values, it will automatically cause us to be angry to varying degrees. Different words that come from the 'anger tree' are: hurt, disappointment, mad, ticked off, depression (anger turned inward), rageful, upset, etc. If you love dogs and you see someone hitting their or somebody else's dog, you're likely to get angry. When a close is in the throes of addiction, when someone lies to you, and when someone doesn't keep their word are all examples of a violation of our values. You might notice feelings of anger, resentment, and disrespect when someone violates one of your values.

Often, we compromise our values as well. We might go too far in physical intimacy on the first date just because the other person asked to, even though we didn't want to. Another example is allowing someone to do things to you that you don't like and getting drunk when you don't drink are examples of a compromised self-esteem/value system. All of the above cause anger and instability. In today's world, this happens more than just on a personal or social level. There are all sorts of global, political, and systemic violations of values going on. For instance, a source of much of the anger and hatred a lot of us feel right now is the direct result of our rights, beliefs, and values being violated or compromised by those in power. Of course, the anger doesn't justify acts of violence. We are still responsible for our decision-making and how we channel that anger productively.

When our self-esteem is threatened, we will be rightly angry. Ever have that hairstyle that you personally love but just doesn't fit into the office setting, and your coworkers don't beat the bush about it? Being laughed at, called names, bullying, and experiencing putdowns are examples of when our self-esteem is attacked. These attacks don't have to be intentional; they just have to be there. Sometimes, our perception of getting mistreated will make us feel the same way when someone mistreats us intentionally. Many biracial children or BIPOC children experience these attacks.

This mistreatment adds to their ongoing struggle with their identity of where they fit in. Many biracial/BIPOC teenagers experience much in the way of 'subtle' ridicule or discrimination in our schools. There's also systemic discrimination that a lot of BIPOC awaken to when they first go to school. Unfortunately, this bullying affects our children's self-worth, makes them depressed, and sometimes leads to suicide. An attack on our self-esteem often happens when people want us to fit into their world and don't accept that we have a world of our own, too. It happens whenever people try to deny our individuality. Everyone has a culture that should be celebrated and not ridiculed, put down, or subjected to conforming to certain societal norms.

Reflection Prompts

- List three ways you incorporate faith into your daily life. How do they strengthen your walk with God?

- Reflect on a time when living out your values brought joy or clarity.

- Write about how the "Fruit of the Spirit" is evident in your life. Which fruits do you want to nurture more?

<u>CHAPTER: 10</u>

<u>SERMON</u>

II Corinthians 5:1-9

For We know that if the earthly tent We live in is destroyed, We have a building from God, an eternal house in heaven, not built by human hands. Meanwhile, We groan, longing to be clothed instead with our heavenly dwelling, because when We are clothed, We will not be found naked. For while We are in this tent, We groan and are burdened because We do not wish to be unclothed but to be clothed instead with our heavenly dwelling so that what is mortal may be swallowed up by life. Now, the one who has fashioned us for this very purpose is God, who has given us the Spirit as a deposit, guaranteeing what is to come. Therefore, We are always confident and know that as long as We are at home in the body, We are away from the Lord. [7] For We live by faith, not by sight. We are confident, I say, and would prefer to be away from the body and at home with the Lord. So We make it our goal to please him, whether We are at home in the body or away from it.

WALKING BY FAITH

I would like for us to look at the concept of a Christian life based on faith. We see many people who claim to have faith. Sadly, when trials come or when things don't go their way, these same people falter in their trust and belief in faith. Jesus said that all you needed was a mustard seed's worth of faith to tell a mountain to move. Faith, in simple terms, is the substance of what we hope for and the evidence of something that is not seen. Substance is things that we can measure, things that we can touch or see. Faith is our substance. I'm not talking about what some folks call blind faith; I'm talking about faith in someone: our Lord Jesus. Faith is also our evidence of things that are not seen. If you see something, can taste something, or can touch something, why would we need faith, right? Our faith is also based on things to come. We know that this is not our final resting place. We know that there is a life to come, and so we put our hope in what our God has told us. We have to include what our brother Paul said in Romans chapter 10: **Faith cometh by hearing, and hearing by the word of God.** So, in order to have faith, we need to have our faith in someone. That someone is, without question or comparison, Jesus: the living word. We need to build our faith on what God has already said in His Word, for we walk by faith. Often, we get sidetracked and start to walk by feelings and not by faith. For some Christians, we have interchanged the two ideas. Faith is not feelings. We often won't move or think God is moving unless we feel a certain way.

We often walk in a way that makes us feel in a certain way. Sometimes, how we feel may dictate how we walk. For instance, someone feeling low may walk with their head down and with a hunched-up posture. On the other hand, someone who wants to exude confidence and wants to be perceived as powerful will walk with their chin high and their shoulders back. I have never seen Jesus, and I think I'm right to assume that none of you have either.

Despite this reality, all of us trust and put our hope in the fact that Jesus is real and that we will be with Him one day. Jesus said that blessed is he who believes who has not seen. We have not seen it, yet we believe it. It is this hope that causes us to keep moving in Jesus' name. The Bible tells us that all we need is just the mustard seed's worth of faith for a mountain to move. "And Jesus said unto them, Because of your unbelief: for verily I say unto you, If ye have faith as a grain of mustard seed, ye shall say unto this mountain, Remove hence to yonder place; and it shall remove, and nothing shall be impossible unto you."

It is not your faith that causes the mountain to move; it is your faith that causes God to move. The Hebrew writer says that without faith, it is impossible to please God. It should be noted that your faith is what causes God to move, and all he needs is a 64th of an inch to do that. It should also be noted that God is pleased when we rely on our faith in Him to move in life. If you find yourself in anxiety or panic, look upwards and seek God's face.

He who has prepared us: God is preparing us right now for our eternal destiny. Our small afflictions and troubles are (in part) how God **has prepared us**. When you are going through a tough time, it is God preparing you. Often, these slight afflictions affect our feelings, which might make you think there is a weakness of faith. I'd like to remind you, though, that our feelings aren't an indication of our level of faith; it is how we continue to walk that does. We need to know that God will, can, and is able. You need to know that God will never leave me nor forsake me. You need to know, and once you know, walk accordingly.

Who has also given us the Spirit as a guarantee: When the earthly life puts us through harsh trials, it isn't always easy to take comfort in our heavenly destiny. It is not always easy to know that we are protected. We are all blessed with the Holy Spirit, who lives in all saints. God knows there are several forces that will constantly distract us, including our feelings. That's why He gave us the Spirit as a guarantee and a guide. He backs up the promise of heaven with a down payment right now, the Holy Spirit. Guarantee is an ancient Greek word that describes a pledge or a partial payment that requires future payments. The one receiving the guarantee has a legal claim to the goods in question.

The Holy Spirit is a part of heaven itself that lives in each of us. The work of the Holy Spirit in us is to grow the bud of heaven. Grace is not a thing that will be taken away from us when we enter glory but will develop into glory. Grace will not be withdrawn as though it had answered its purpose but will be matured into glory.

Therefore, we are always confident: The presence of the Holy Spirit in Paul's life gave him confidence and should give us confidence as well. It assured us that God is at work in us and will continue His work. If you struggle to affirm yourself of your confidence, then ask God for a fresh outpouring of the Holy Spirit in your life. By faith, let God know what you need. We can always be confident, even in hard times, if we remember: Set your mind on things above, not on things on the earth.

For we walk by faith, not by sight: Right now, the presence of God is a matter of faith. We are at home, inside our bodies, so there is a sense in which we are absent from the Lord, at least in the sense of His immediate, glorious presence. So now, We must walk by faith, not by sight. Blessed are those who believe but have not seen. Your feelings don't have sight.

To walk by faith, not by sight, is one of the greatest – yet the most difficult – principles of Christian living. Imagine how amazed must be the angels that we live for, serve, and are willing to die for a God we have never seen. Yet, we love Him and live for Him, living by faith, not by sight. To walk by faith means to make faith part of every daily activity. Walking is nothing remarkable in itself; what's remarkable is walking with faith in the mundane or tedious aspects of life. But God wants us to walk by faith. The day will come when we will no longer be absent from the Lord in the sense that Paul means it here. On that day, We will not have to walk by faith, but We will see the glory and the presence of God.

When hard times come, rely on your faith instead of your feelings. You can acknowledge and regulate your feelings but recognize that your faith is above passing emotions. Your faith comes by hearing and hearing the word of God. Know that your faith has just been increased if you heard this word. Know that your small afflictions are preparing you so you can use the faith that you have. When there's been a big change in your life, whether good or bad, we must remember that God is still in charge and rely on Him. When your feelings are tried and pushed, know that your faith is what matters more to God. God knows how you feel but tells us to rely on our faith when we live. Keep on walking with Jesus, and He will work it out. Know that the battle belongs to the Lord. Know that the joy of the Lord is your strength. Know that your faith, though it is tried, is much more precious than gold. When life throws things at you, it is God who is still in charge. Walk by faith. Work your faith. Use your faith. Walk in your faith. Stand on your faith. Look to God to continue to strengthen your faith.

Reflection Prompts

- What does "faith over fear" mean in your life? Reflect on a situation where faith overcame doubt.

- How do you experience spiritual growth in everyday moments?

- Write about a time when focusing on God brought clarity or peace to a chaotic situation.

(All scriptures taken from Bible Gateway)

Disappointment

I think all of us can benefit from spending a bunch of time with the term disappointment and seeing how significant it can be in the lives of others. Disappointment comes to us in many different forms and at many different stages of life. Maybe we lost a sweetheart, or we didn't get that job the promotion we worked so hard for. We can be disappointed at getting picked last on a basketball team or even at not getting that last piece of chicken at dinner. These disappointments are a part of life and living.

I have learned that this same disappointment can be a catalyst for some enormous disturbances. Many relational arguments start with disappointment. The husband wanted to have sex, and the wife didn't is a popular disappointing situation. Even though it seems frivolous, disappointments like these can lead to anger, arguments, and, sometimes, domestic violence. Did you see what happened, though? It started with there being an expectation that wasn't met.

Many times, the expectation wasn't met because it remained unclear or unspoken. When the expectation is clear to one and not to the other person, it remains unclear. To steer clear of disappointments, both people in a relationship have to agree and communicate effectively. Another common problem that disappointment can cause has to do with pornography. This, I am convinced, is the #1 item that causes a continuation of porn in the life of men and women. It may start with a look, and the feeling and thoughts can grow to become bigger than life. The person often becomes disappointed and guilt-ridden that the 'temptation' happened. They are often mad that it came to their mind as if being tempted is a 'sin'. Jesus was tempted all the time, yet without sin.

The temptation is not the issue. It is yielding to the temptation that is the problem. Many men, especially, may have the belief that they are ONLY supposed to be attracted to their wives, so they aren't supposed to be 'excited' when they see an attractive woman. It seems to be all right if some ladies talk about how a guy looks at the checkout stand in the supermarket. God has made some beautiful people in the world. That is not the issue.

The issue is when you try to make somebody else YOURS. Isn't that what Eve did in the Garden? When guys are disappointed for having the thoughts and the temptations, they tend to beat themselves up and find themselves right in front of a computer screen, looking for a woman to help them with their disappointment. If these men thought ahead, they would realize that guilt and shame are waiting on the other side of the computer screen. They would realize that succumbing to this 'episode' further solidifies their self-directed disappointment. So, they may even walk around with the attitude of disappointment before anything ever happens that day. When 'something' does happen, they go down that path that the disappointment leads them to, which is sex with someone who isn't there to ease the disappointment that is there.

When there is disappointment, the first thing that comes to mind is that there is a void.

That void can become quite haunting because you know that something is missing and there's not much you can do about it. I believe that this void is the love that is missing and the love that we yearn for. The person often believes that because there is a void and because they are not loved, affirmed, or validated, they are worthless. They may also believe that they're not good enough, that they are a burden, or that no one cares about them. Their thoughts then continue to do whatever they can to try to fill the void. So, that is when substitutes for love are found. Substitutes or things like drugs, alcohol, gambling, and pornography are all self-defeating behaviors that do more harm than good for that gaping void.

Other things that can come up to fill this void are loneliness, despair, rejection, anxiety, and depression, all coming from disappointment. Disappointment in itself is not bad. We're often disappointed at our football team that may have lost at the last minute. We may become disappointed that we didn't get the job that we wanted. We may be disappointed that the love of our life has decided to go with someone else. So, disappointment is not necessarily a bad thing. It is how we handle the disappointment that can often lead to maladaptive behaviors.

When disappointment comes knocking at your door, the best solution is to remember the baseline of who you are. I have often asked people in my sessions to name five things that will never change about them. I have to remind them that weight and hair color do not count. You'd be surprised to find out how many people have a difficult time coming up with just five. Some have two long drives. I do this exercise because when people can determine unchanging things about their character, they can have their opportunity and a better chance of overcoming disappointment. Some examples of unchanging things or defining character traits are honesty, trustworthiness, kindness, determination, courage, love, care, peace, and faith. It is important to know that these character traits are the items that we typically use to make decisions in life, as well as to guide how we live life itself. If we can hold on to them during tumultuous times, then no matter how many disappointments come, we'll be able to handle them. For those of us who are Christians, these are the fruit of the spirit which are our godly character traits.

Did you notice how none of these character traits are emotions? God never created our emotions to be our decision-makers nor to be our guide in life. Our emotions are an expression or a reaction to something that just happened in our life. We should typically leave it that way since the part of our body that was made to make decisions is our brain, and if we let emotions linger, the brain will be too clouded to make the right decisions.

I am not saying we can't be emotional. We just can't let our emotions be our decision-makers. For instance, When I was in my bed this morning, it felt really, really cozy. I did not want to go out of bed at all. I was comfortable, so why would I? It felt as if four to five arms were holding me down in the bed, telling me to stay there! I'm sure the same thing happens to you, too. But my brain told me that I needed to get up to go to work. In moments like these, I'm glad I don't use my emotions to make that choice! If I'd relied solely on my emotions, I may have been out of a job.

<u>Feelings</u>

Feelings are great and peculiar at the same time. Initially, feelings occur because something 'just' happened. But as a secondary response, when we initially feel something, we may associate it with our past. We may become triggered to remember painful memories of our past, but the initial feelings are because something just happened. Many times, when we start feeling, we are pushed to our past because we want to change it or the future because we want to control the circumstances. Because of our pasts, we can be influenced to translate the meaning of our feelings differently than what they are.

Many couples struggle with feelings. Let us remember that a couple or a family is an emotional system. We humans comprise different systems, including the respiratory system and the circularity system, which are themselves both made of many parts. Similarly, a couple and a family are the parts of an emotional system. Almost everything done is emotional/relational first.

Most couples believe that a certain situation is the cause of their emotional outbursts. What they don't realize is that it's not because of any situation but because of the emotional system that is attacked, pushed, rubbed the wrong way, or misunderstood. My mother used to tell me, "Never make a permanent decision based on a temporary situation because all situations are temporary." One time, I was listening to a Christian radio station, and I heard two people talking about couple communication.

They stated that communicating is hard between couples. I totally disagree with that premise. I don't think it's the communication that is hard, but the willingness to understand the communication that is often difficult. People aren't willing to put their egos or emotional hurts behind and try to understand the other person. It's indeed true that you can communicate all you want, but if the other person doesn't have the capacity to understand you, it doesn't matter how well you communicate.

The communication is often filled with and laced with that person's point of view, their past, their biases and their preferences. Most times, we have an already predetermined meaning to our emotions. Many folks believe that it is wrong, evil, inappropriate, or unsafe to be anxious. They try to get rid of the 'feeling' of being anxious. People even believe that the anxiety is because something bad is coming, something wrong is going to happen. When they try to get rid of the feeling, they actually make the feelings more intense. When you try to stop something, you actually end up doing that thing you are trying to stop. God tells us to walk in the spirit, and we will not fulfill the lusts of the flesh.

CHAPTER:11

THE BENEFIT OF BEING VULNERABLE

IN A RELATIONSHIP

Most definitions of the word vulnerable talk about a person being susceptible to harm and being in a position where other people can hurt you. In a relationship, it may refer to expressing parts of yourself that you are least confident, find embarrassing, or believe that part of you is a deterrent to how your mate views you. This definition may carry the thought of being attacked, let down, put down, and caused to be put or seen into a position that will cause partial or permanent distance in the relationship.

In all actuality, being vulnerable is an essential part of a strong and successful relationship. It is virtually impossible to be loved by someone or to love someone unless you allow yourself to be vulnerable on purpose. It is the vulnerability that allows love to grow and to be expressed at its maximum capacity. Being vulnerable allows trust to be experienced at a high level. You may have to surrender some perceived control, but the benefits are well worth this control. Of course, this 'type' of vulnerability gradually develops in a relationship as a process. Being vulnerable isn't something that just 'happens'. Of course, letting people in or being vulnerable is a very risky endeavor. You're putting the most fragile parts of yourself in somebody's hand and hoping they accept them instead of using them to hurt you. But, as is with most good things in life, every close relationship comes with risks. I remember how my mother would tell me that no one really *has* to love me. It's more of a choice than a demand. It is a choice that someone makes towards you and you towards them. So, the fact that someone has chosen to love you and be loved by you is very honoring.

With this honoring exchange, someone ought to be grateful enough to say 'thank you'. What makes love so great is that love and trust happen with a choice and with feelings. Love and trust are 'conjoined twins'; one can't have one without the other. When you see one, you see the other in practice.

What are some daily things that are associated with being vulnerable? Being able to share your current feelings is one. Marriage is an 'emotional system'. Every action a couple does with, towards, or around each other is emotional /relational first. When a couple looks at each other, it is an emotional experience; not sometimes, not most time, but every time. It may be an increase in anger or a loving thought or feeling, but it is emotional. It can feel 'weird' to share our current feelings just because we are feeling them. Each couple wants to be able to share their current feelings with their partner with the hope of still being accepted in a positive light. The idea of feelings used refers to actual 'emotions'. Feelings, which are used interchangeably with the term emotions, include anger, joy, happiness, disappointment, sadness, depression, loneliness, excitement, anxiety, uneasiness, etc.

Often, couples use the phrase "I feel that" or "I feel like" to express something about themselves. These are **_NOT_** feelings but thoughts that the person has who expressed the phrase. How does 'like' feel? How does 'that' feel? Often, people use these phrases to justify their position, a thought, or an opinion. These phrases are used to state items that the speaker expresses with the belief that the expressed 'feeling' should not be questioned or challenged because the word 'feel like' or 'feel that' is included.

However convincing they may seem, these phrases do not have any merit to justify a position of emotion. They're base is an opinion stated, usually, about the current situation. These phrases can get couples in trouble as they can lead to arguments on opinions. They may be a way to express frustration, fear, loneliness, or abandonment. These phrases can also be used to defend a position so that they protect themselves from being vulnerable with their mate. These phrases don't allow an effort to create closeness to be effective. Opinions are not typically used to cause connection but more so an attempt to cause agreement so that the potential of conflict goes down. Those two can often be different.

Typically, the difficulty in sharing feelings can cause feelings of uneasiness, which can lead to thoughts of being vulnerable. Often, people have a predetermined definition of their feelings. Vulnerable often accompanies the feeling of being uneasy. Uneasy can carry a 'negative' connotation of something bad is about to happen, I'm not safe, it is wrong to feel uneasy, I have to get away, a reminder that I am in a bad place. Remember the phrase that is often used in Star Wars, "I have a bad feeling about this." If this is the definition of feeling uneasy, it will be avoided at all costs. The same can be said of the emotion of 'anxiety', which has a similar definition for many people. Of course, this aforementioned definition of anxiety and unease appears to be more prominent in people who have a history of betrayal, trauma, abandonment, and physical or emotional mistreatment. If this is the case, the reaction to being anxious becomes a 'sympathetic' reaction.

In this state, a 'flight or fight' reaction takes place. The fight-or-flight or the fight-flight-freeze-or-fawn is also known in scientific terms as hyperarousal or the acute stress response. It is a physiological reaction that is our body's response to a perceived harmful event, attack, or threat to survival. The fight-or-flight response is characterized by an increased heart rate, anxiety, increased perspiration, tremor, and increased blood glucose. These physiological effects co-occur with neural or hormonal responses to stress, such as increases in corticotropin and cortisol (the stress hormone) secretion.

The reaction to the emotions becomes a physical reaction and, over time, can be automatic or autonomic. The sympathetic (part of the autonomic nervous system) functions like a car's gas pedal. When you perceive something as threatening, it triggers the fight-or-flight response, providing the body with a burst of energy so that it can respond to perceived danger. That means there is no thought to the reaction, and the 'flight or flight' reaction of the nervous system dominates. The mind, then, has little to no control over the ability to process the emotion as the body has already made the decision based on preconceived notions from the past. There is little to no chance of emotional connection at this point, as the emotions from the past are flooding the brain. The possibility of vulnerabiltiy, which in essence is the opportunity of hurt and pain, becomes real. Then, this reaction appears only justified. When this reaction occurs in a present relationship, it can birth 'fear' of openness and vulnerability. However, it is really not an emotion; it is a belief system. Just like all 'phobias,' there's a set of beliefs behind this fear. Fear of vulnerability inhibits the partner from displaying relational emotions like peace, safety, security, closeness, softness, and joy. Instead, the partner can feel hurt and pain because of the emotions of unease and anxiety that typically accompany vulnerability. The fight-or-flight reaction becomes real and energized with this predetermined definition and the reaction mentioned above.

The perception of unease and anxiety has to be inaccurate since they aren't based on reality but on a preconceived belief of impending doom, hurt, and pain. Let's consider the daily life experiences that cause uneasiness: an exam, traffic, dentist, illness, public speaking, an unfamiliar place, a first kiss. All of these induce a normal and healthy anxiety reaction. Feeling anxious in such situations isn't bad, wrong, or unsafe. In fact, it would be unusual not to feel uneasy in these everyday moments. Many preconceived notions can feel valid because they stem from historical events, but relying on phrases like 'I feel like' or 'I feel that' can reinforce distorted thinking and the unsafe feelings that arise.

Do you know what the goal should be when there's an opportunity to talk about your feelings? The goal should be staying in the present and dealing with what is happening in the 'here and now'. Take it as an opportunity to talk about your experience and share feelings, fears, and opinions in the present. Remember what we discussed earlier? That the present is the only place where decisions are made, trust is experienced, and love is demonstrated. There is no other time but the present when being vulnerable can be experienced in a safe and loving manner. The past exists with its predetermined definition, opinions, thoughts, and beliefs. If we allow it, it can distort and cause havoc in the present.

Vulnerability needs to be a mutually consented and agreed-upon act with the purpose of increasing trust in a relationship. When you're allowing someone to see your heart through communicating heartfelt emotions, the other party is responsible for understanding the source and reason of these feelings. A person who is sharing their feelings with you would not be sharing their feelings with the intent of causing pain to the receiver. On the contrary, it is an attempt to face their fear of vulnerability in order to connect.

This is how it must be received:

- Both partners are able to share historical hurts, pains, and regrets by the partner or others in previous relationships or childhood.

- Both partners are able to share their opinions without the 'fear' of being criticized, accused, or put down. One has to be mindful not to get defensive here.

- Being willing to show positive emotions around your partner or express physical affection. For many people, these actions can also feel scary, exposing, or even triggering.

- Being vulnerable can sometimes simply mean telling someone you care about them or even just hugging them.

"Dear reader, I pray that some of the tools mentioned in this book can help you on your life's journey as you go through all the trials and 'junk' that surrounds us. It is so important that we all keep working and navigating all the unpredictable things—the good and the bad—that life brings us. Keep walking through the pain, heartache, and unpredictability of life. Find someone you can trust and who is willing to walk with you and you with them.

When you feel disheartened and let down by life, remember Joshua. Joshua came to the Throne carrying many wounds, scars, heartaches, and brokenness, and yet, he kept striving towards to Throne and let God—via Jesus—be his healer, provider, protector, strength bearer, and as my mother would say: his "leaning post."

If you've come this far in the book, know that you've given me encouragement. I pray and have faith that something you read in these few pages has motivated you to keep on striving. If you want to share your thoughts about my book or want to reach, I would love to hear from you at my work email, which is drdshootsllc@gmail.com. "